Thomas
A Lifetime Denied

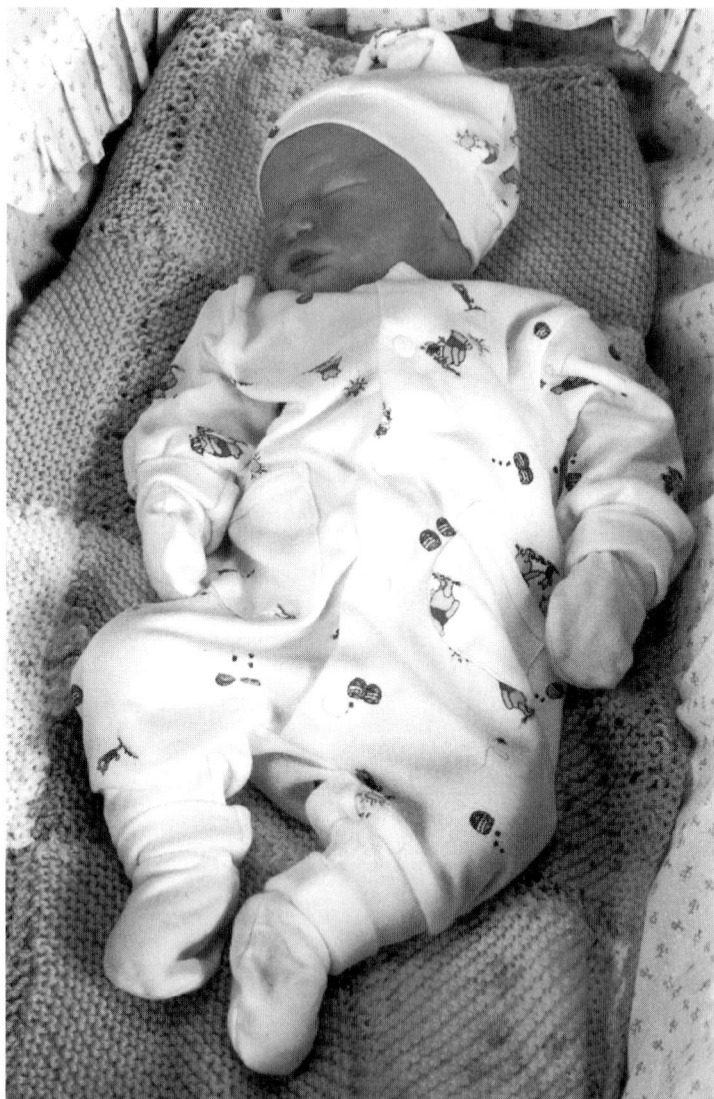

Thomas
We planned to bring him home
from the hospital in this outfit.

Thomas

A Lifetime Denied

Shelley Wilkinson

Sands
Stillbirth & neonatal death charity

Published by Bosun-Publications
The Ferry Point
Ferry Lane
Shepperton on Thames
TW17 9LQ

Tel: 01932 787151

First published in Great Britain in 2007
by Bosun-Publications on behalf of
Sands, the stillbirth and neonatal death charity
28 Portland Place
London W1B 1LY

Tel: 020 7436 7940
Helpline: 020 7436 5881
Email: support@uk-sands.org
Website: www.uk-sands.org

ISBN: 0-9554243-1-3
ISBN: 978-0-9554243-1-1

Thomas - A Lifetime Denied. Copyright © 2007 Shelley Wilkinson

A CIP catalogue record for this book is available from the British Library.
Typeset in 12pt Minion
Printed in England by
The Cromwell Press Ltd

Book design and production by
FW Barter ARCA
Bosun-Publications
Email: fbarter@bosun-press.demon.co.uk

Contents   Page

Dedication

*First and foremost, this book
is dedicated to my baby,
Thomas James William Wilkinson,
who passed through my life too quickly,
but touched my heart forever.*

*This book is also dedicated to the seventeen babies a day
who are either stillborn or die soon after birth.
You live on in all our hearts.*

*Whilst waiting for the publication of this book,
my beloved Nana has passed away. I just hope
that wherever she is, she knows how much I love her.
I hope with all my heart
that she and Thomas have been reunited.*

Nana – Did you ever know that you're my hero?

Acknowledgement

I would like to thank my husband, Stephen. From the moment we first met, I knew we would be together forever. You are my soul mate.

I would also like to thank my precious children, Holly and Joe. You both give me the strength to live in such a hostile world. Holly, you gave me the will to survive when Thomas died. Joe, you gave me back something that was so cruelly denied.

To my parents and my in-laws, you all eased my pain with your support and help. Mum and Dad, you gave me life and helped make the woman I am today. I love you both!

Sue and Derek, you are like my second Mum and Dad, thank you!

Nana, there isn't and never will be another lady like you. I love you and respect you.

To my brother and sister, we are so close and I cherish you both.

Ragen, my friend and confidant, you are a calm influence on my life, much more than you can ever know.

Adrienne, an inspirational woman who is a dedicated friend to those in distress. We all thank you.

To the rest of my family, it would take ages to mention you all by name. Thank you!

Finally, my thanks go to Sands. The Stillbirth and neonatal death charity, especially Neal Long, for believing in me and giving me the opportunity to tell the world about my beautiful baby boy, Thomas.

Foreword

There can be very few more shocking experiences during a pregnancy than a placental abruption. In this situation, part or all of the placenta becomes detached from the wall of the uterus, and because of the presence of the baby within the uterus, the uterine muscles are unable to contract and thus clamp off the exposed blood vessels, so leading to sudden, frequently torrential blood loss, extreme pain and shock. The death of the baby is almost inevitable. Occasionally the mother dies too. It is a true obstetric emergency.

When I met Shelley for the first time, it was 8 a.m. on the morning after she had suffered the death of her second child, Thomas, through just the event I have described. Seemingly, by the time the people caring for her had become aware of what was happening, Thomas was dead, and Shelley was profoundly shocked. Her condition had to be stabilised before it was safe to deliver the baby by caesarean section.

As I entered the room on the delivery suite that morning, Shelley began to beg and plead with me to 'do something'. Her baby had died, she cried, because no-one had listened. She herself describes those few hours very graphically in the pages of this book.

Over the next few weeks and months, I came to know Shelley very well. We met weekly, and I grew to admire her strength and fortitude, and her determination to ensure that this should never happen again to anyone else. She refused to be patronised or allow her concerns to be brushed aside, remaining firm and dignified throughout. She earned the admiration and respect of everyone she met during the course of the next year, particularly as she decided to return to her studies immediately instead of taking a year out as planned - no small feat while coping with huge sadness and loss, at the same time as pursuing her investigation into Thomas's death

We developed a strong, trusting relationship which has never been dented. Over six years, I have seen Shelley grow emotionally and psychologically. I have seen her change the direction of her life and shared with her the satisfaction of her amazing academic success. Best of all, I have shared with her the birth of Joe, Thomas's little brother. She is never afraid to talk about Thomas and what his death meant, and still means, to her and her family.

She was instrumental in helping me to establish the Parents' Support Group, which I facilitate. At one particular memorable meeting, Shelley was able to say that she now accepted that she would not see Thomas again, but he was held safe within her heart for ever. She also felt that she had so much to thank him for, because if he hadn't died, she would never know Joe, and this little boy has brought her so much pleasure and happiness.

Shelley is a remarkable woman, and it has been a privilege for me to have been beside her through the worst times and the best.

Adrienne (Bereavement Support Midwife)

Chapter 1

The summer of the year 2000 was such a special time for Stephen and I. It marked the beginning of a whole new chapter in our lives. I was nearing the end of my pregnancy with our second child and had just finished the first year of an undergraduate course in Humanities. Finding out I was having another baby had been a huge surprise to us, but we looked on this new life as a blessing, and we called it our miracle baby. To us, the baby was just meant to be. As soon as we knew he existed he was very much wanted and loved and I would sit for hours reading both university text books and baby magazines. Each evening I would give Stephen a running commentary of what stage in its development our baby had reached. Our daughter, Holly, fixed a chart to her bedroom wall and would cross off the days until our baby's arrival.

Unfortunately, the last few weeks of my pregnancy had been plagued by complications, which had necessitated admission to hospital on a number of occasions and the 17th July was no exception. That morning I had been shopping with my sister to buy some last minute things for the baby. In the afternoon my community midwife paid me a visit; I had been having daily visits for the previous three days. As I was showing physiological signs of the potentially life threatening condition pre-eclampsia, which included raised blood pressure, protein in my urine, swelling of my face, fingers and ankles and visual disturbances, I was sent for observation to the Foetal Assessment Unit at my local hospital. On entering the unit, I had resigned myself to the fact that yet again I would be spending another night in hospital. However, when entering the hospital, I had started to feel a trickle of what I assumed to be my amniotic fluid leaking and as I was now thirty-nine weeks pregnant, I was confident that the next time I left the hospital I would be holding our much wanted and very anticipated newborn baby. Convinced that labour was imminent, I informed the midwife on duty of my situation but after being examined I was told that no liquor, which is the clinical name for the amniotic fluid which surrounds the baby within the womb, could be seen. Twenty minutes later I was placed on a cardiotocography machine, which is used to externally monitor the unborn baby's heart rate. My baby was very active at this time and although the transducer kept losing contact with his heartbeat, I was reassured by the midwife that all was well and a reactive trace had been obtained. I did not realise how precious my time spent on that monitor was to become to me in the following months; it was the last time I was ever to hear the steady beat of my precious baby's heart. Soon my baby was to be snatched away from me forever.

Although at that point it appeared all was well with the baby, I was still advised to stay on the antenatal unit overnight for observation. The decision to entrust my life and the life of my unborn baby into the care of the midwifery team, was a decision that would change my life forever. I never imagined that when I finally left the hospital, my life would never be the same again.

Even now, six years later, when I see the evening summer sun streaming through our windows, I am transported back to the summer of 2000, especially to the evening of Monday the 17th July, when I was in Room 2 on Ward C3. My recollection of that evening is burned into my memory forever. That night feels like a lifetime away but also feels like it happened yesterday. If I let my mind drift back to that evening, I can still vividly remember how any feelings of excitement at the prospect of being in early labour were soon replaced by feelings of fear and apprehension, when within hours the pain I was experiencing in my lower abdomen and back increased in such severity that I began to question whether something was wrong. Many pregnant women have an idealised view of how their labour will be and I was no exception but what unfolded that evening was anything but ideal, it was an absolute nightmare.

At 8:30 pm, a midwife performed a further trace of the baby's heart rate using a Pinnard stethoscope, which is a trumpet-shaped listening device. She reported a normal and healthy heart rate of 140 - 160 beats per minute. It was at this point that I told her I was still experiencing pains in my lower abdomen and I also felt nauseous. She suggested various reasons for the pain and sickness, but like earlier, appeared unconvinced that I was in early labour. By nine o'clock I had begun to feel more nauseous and generally unwell. I also began to lose more amniotic fluid. I visited the midwives' office, as I felt they were being flippant in recognising I was in the early stages of labour. I was told they were performing a handover to the night shift midwife and she would come to see me when they were finished. On returning to my room, the pains which had initially felt like mild period cramps, became progressively worse. I began to feel lethargic and decided to lie on my bed and wait for the midwife to come. As I lay alone in my room, darkness came and sometime between nine o'clock and nine thirty, an auxiliary nurse entered the room. I told her I felt I was going to be sick and she placed a sick bowl on my bed. At nine thirty the night shift midwife, who I will refer to as 'Midwife A', entered my room. I explained my situation to her, telling her the pain was at this point still bearable but getting progressively worse. She checked my blood pressure and pulse, agreed I probably was in the first stages of labour and informed me she would retrieve a CTG machine, in order to perform a further heart trace. With that she left the room. It was from that point that the pain became more and more unbearable. I had never actually experienced contractions before, as my daughter had been born by elective caesarean section, but somehow alarm bells began to ring and I began to fear that something was wrong. The pain I was experiencing was continuous, it did not come and go like I had expected, it just seemed to increase in magnitude. Ten minutes later I was relieved to see Midwife A return but she went into the room next to mine and became engaged in a lengthy conversation with a patient. I became very frightened and distressed. I desperately wanted to attract her attention but the nurse call button was high on the wall, out of my reach. I felt too weak to move or even call out to attract her attention. Finally, when she emerged from the room, twenty minutes later, I managed to call out and attract her attention. I informed her of how much pain I was experiencing and a number of times I told her I was starting to panic as the pain was so severe and not easing – it was just one long continuous contraction. The midwife made me feel I was getting all worked up about nothing. I was fearful that something was seriously wrong but she managed to convince me that what I was experiencing was the normal first stages of labour. She decided to perform an internal examination, to check the condition of my cervix and assess how far along my labour was. It was during this examination that I realised that the fluid that was draining from my body was not clear amniotic fluid like earlier, but was in fact blood. When I realised I was bleeding, I really began to panic and

I repeatedly asked the midwife if it was normal to lose blood when in labour, to which she replied, "It can be."

Whilst being examined I was in sheer agony. I was finding it hard to keep still and found myself writhing on the bed in pain. I told the midwife that if I needed any other examinations, I would require some form of pain relief first. She informed me that she would ring the delivery suite and if they were not busy, they would send someone to collect me and I would be able to have some pain medication. I asked her to call Stephen, who was at home with our daughter. She said she would, then left the room, closing the door behind her. Although I was bleeding and she had performed an internal examination, Midwife A did not attempt to monitor my baby's heart rate. It has always been my opinion that had she done so, Thomas, the name we gave our baby boy, may have been showing signs of foetal distress and an emergency caesarean performed.

Stephen arrived at 10:15 pm, after taking our excited daughter to stay at her aunt's house. "Tomorrow you will meet your new baby brother or sister," he told her.

From the time Midwife A left, to Stephen arriving, I spent thirty minutes in horrific pain. I felt so alone, frightened and isolated. On entering my room, Stephen found me lying on my right side, crying in pain. Straight away I told him something was wrong and I was fearful for our baby, as I had not felt him move for a while. I asked him to see if I was still bleeding. He told me I was. He recalls the tops of my legs were covered in blood, as was the sheet upon which I lay. Soon after, Midwife A entered the room, accompanied by a midwife from the delivery suite. They told me I needed to get off the bed into a wheelchair, to enable them to transport me to the delivery suite. I told them I was in too much pain and unable to move. I pleaded with them to take me on the bed. They refused. I was helped off the bed and they walked me to the chair, at the same time, blood was oozing down my legs onto the floor. It was only when they finally sat me in the chair that they both became alarmed at the blood loss and realised I needed immediate transfer to the delivery suite. For some reason they made me get back out of the chair and took me back to the bed. Making my way back to the bed, I found myself slipping in my own blood which now covered the floor.

Chapter 2

When I reached the delivery suite, things began to happen very quickly. The room became a hive of activity as doctors were crash bleeped and midwives frantically attempted to locate the baby's heartbeat. While all this was going on around me, the pain still increased. It was like a horrific burning sensation which radiated outwards from my womb. My abdomen was also getting bigger, as it was filling with blood faster than it could drain away. Many times I thought I was going to die and I can still recall Stephen asking, "What's happening, what's wrong?"

Stephen was stood by my side when we entered the room but as time passed, he appeared to sink further and further away, until he was standing in the corner, with his head in his hands.

I was attached to various machines to monitor my condition and the staff tried both internally and externally to find the baby's heartbeat. When my main organs began to shut down, I was given two large bore intravenous drips, to rapidly replace fluids in an effort to stop my body slipping further into hypovolaemic shock. Strangely, I almost forgot I was heavily pregnant but I was quickly reminded when the consultant obstetrician turned to me, looked me in the eyes and said, "Shelley, we are almost certain your baby has died."

I remember hearing Stephen begin to cry and myself screaming, "No, no, no – not my baby!"

A radiographer was called in, to perform an ultrasound scan to confirm the baby had died. When she placed the transducer upon my abdomen, the pain was excruciating but I managed to turn to look at the screen and saw a profile of our baby. I knew he was dead; there was no waving, kicking or wriggling, like previous scans, but a deathly stillness. He was gone.

Knowing the baby was dead, the staff turned all their attention to stabilising my condition. They couldn't stop the bleeding and I needed to go to theatre for an emergency caesarean section. It was at this point that I started to ask for my mum. I needed my mum more than any other time in my entire life. I knew she was somewhere in the hospital, as Stephen had telephoned her to tell her I was in labour before he left our house.

In the waiting room of the maternity unit my mum and Stephen's mum were waiting for news of the arrival of their newest grandchild. They were led into a private room on the delivery suite and told there had been complications and the baby had died. Devastated, my mum ran out into the corridor looking for me, closely followed by my mother-in-law. Amidst the pain and commotion, I recall hearing a voice at the door of my room shouting, "Is that my daughter? Is that Shelley?"

"Mum!" I cried.

She came over to me and I said, "It's gone mum. The baby's gone."

"I know sweetheart," she said through her sobs. The shock of seeing her eldest daughter surrounded by medical staff, as they fought to save her life, will stay with my mum forever. I was horribly bloated and a dirty yellow colour. She said I was only recognisable by my bright blue eyes.

At some point during the ordeal, I reached a point where the pain appeared to subside. Maybe it was my body releasing a rush of endorphins or maybe I had start-ed to give up my fight for survival. I began to ask if I could go home. Like an injured animal, I wanted to go home to the comfort of my familiar surroundings. I recall crying out, "God help me," to which I heard a voice reply, "God can't help you now Shelley."

I have never found out who said those words to me. I believe it was my subconscious telling me that I had to fight this nightmare alone. Soon, more members of my family arrived and the sight which met them will haunt them forever. They were devastated to see a nine month pregnant woman arching her back and gurgling in unbearable pain. At this point, I was still bleeding profusely and the midwives were constantly mopping blood off me, off the bed and off the floor.

Eventually, three hours after my nightmare began, my condition was stabilised sufficiently enough for my body to withstand a general anaesthetic and I was prepared for theatre and wheeled down to the anaesthetic room. Stephen came with me as far as he could. Before they took me through, we just looked at each other. Stephen and I are soul mates; we did not need words at that moment. Finally, in the operating theatre my fight for survival kicked in and I begged them not to let me die. I told them I had a six-year-old daughter waiting for me at home. I told them how much she needed me.

We needed to wait for extra cross-matched blood to be brought from the blood bank, and even though the obstetrician assured me it was en route, I was in so much pain that I pleaded with them to begin without the blood, but they couldn't. Eventually, it arrived and the anaesthetist explained to me that as it was an emergency caesarean, and I had eaten only hours earlier, they would need to squeeze my throat closed as I slipped under the anaesthetic. I became very frightened and asked if someone would hold my hand as I went to sleep. At that point I really did not know if I would survive the operation. I was lying completely flat, and could not see who it was, but I felt a warm hand clasp mine. I wish to thank whoever that hand belonged to. Just before they began the operation, I looked to my left and glimpsed sight of a resussitaire unit. These are used for babies who need special care at the point of delivery. I knew it would be of no use to my baby. I knew it was too late. Just as had been explained to me, I felt a hand tighten against my throat and within seconds I was asleep. At 01:09 am on the 18th July, 2000, whilst I lay in a state of induced unconsciousness, our baby son was stillborn, weighing seven pounds fourteen ounces, measuring fifty-five centimetres in length and sporting a mass of brown hair and a dimple in his chin. The second part of my nightmare had just begun.

Chapter 3

In a relative's room in the delivery suite, Stephen and our mums waited for news. As other members of our families arrived, they were ushered into the room. From speaking with my family, I know that in the room, most of the people who had seen me suffering, did not think I was going to survive the operation. Eventually, after what must have seemed like hours, my consultant entered the room, still dressed in his green scrubs. He told my family that I had survived the operation, but I was still very poorly. He went on to say that the baby had not survived. Someone in the room asked if the baby was a boy or a girl. When the consultant said he was a baby boy, Stephen and the rest of our family let out a cry of grief. Stephen's first born son had died. The son that he had dreamed of taking to football matches, playing remote control cars with, and taking to the pub on his eighteenth birthday for his first legal pint, was dead.

The first thing I remember, after coming round from the anaesthetic, was seeing my consultant. I asked him if the baby had been delivered. He told me it had. I then asked if it was a boy or a girl. I was told it was a little boy. Finally I asked, "Is he alive?"

The consultant said I had grown and nurtured a perfect baby boy but unfortunately he had been deprived of oxygen and had died. Still drowsy from the anaesthetic, I must have drifted back to sleep because the next thing I remember is opening my eyes and seeing Stephen and my parents. Like any daughter, I always turned to my dad for help and advice. When I saw him sitting there, I thought everything would be alright. If anyone could help me, he could.

"Dad," I said, "Please help me, please make him better."

My dad gripped my hand and told me, in his calm and soothing voice that if there was anything he could do to bring my baby back to me and ease my pain, he would, but he couldn't. That summer day, in the early hours of the morning, my dad tried to help me face the fact that there was nothing anyone could do to help me. He admitted that the coming months would be hard, but he told me I must face my grief and pain and be strong. At first, in the early days, I did not think my dad was right, I could not believe that my baby was dead but as time went on, I realised how true his words were. Dad, I love you for your honesty and wisdom.

Over the next few hours, I found it hard to believe that I was the mother of a dead baby. No parent ever dreams they will outlive any of their children. I kept thinking and hoping that a midwife would come in and tell me that a mistake had been made and in fact the baby was alive, but nobody did. I was asked if I wanted to dress the baby myself or would I prefer it if a member of staff dressed him. I declined to dress him, a decision which even today, I deeply regret. I was so frightened; I thought he would be cold and stiff. How wrong I was. He was dressed in an outfit we had planned to take him home in. It was a cream 'Winnie the Pooh' babygrow, with a matching hat and it was a perfect fit. When he was brought into the room, my mum reached into the Moses basket and as she placed him into my open arms she whispered, "Here he is Shelley. Here's your baby, he's beautiful."

He was so beautiful, he took my breath away. He was not cold or stiff; he was very pale in colour, but he was warm and cuddly. He was just perfect. I held him to my chest and rocked him, saying over and over, "My baby's dead, my baby's dead."

Soon, more members of our families began to arrive. Each one was consumed by sheer grief at the sight of this perfect, but dead baby. Everyone took turns to hold him. We all rocked him and kissed him. We told him how much we loved him and would never forget him. Thousands of silent tears were shed that morning and the immense sorrow in that room was completely overwhelming, but there was also a serene calmness. Here we were, nursing the most beautiful and peaceful looking baby, in the presence of something so pure and so innocent, hysterical wailing and screaming would have been so out of place. Stephen and I asked if we could have him christened, but unfortunately as he was stillborn we could only be offered a blessing, performed by the hospital chaplain. We both agreed, willing to accept any recognition of his being and the chance to formally give him the names we had chosen for him. And so, at 06:30 am, laid in his mummy's arms and surrounded by his family, our son was blessed and given the names Thomas James William Wilkinson.

After the blessing, I began to ask what had happened to me. My consultant explained that I had suffered a massive placental abruption. An abruption occurs when the placenta prematurely detaches from the uterine wall. It is a medical emergency which requires swift action to prevent the death of the pregnant woman and the unborn child. As the placenta detaches, the baby becomes deprived of oxygen and if it is not delivered quickly, severe hypoxia occurs, resulting in brain damage or death. For the woman, there are problems relating to severe blood loss, such as clinical shock. If left untreated, she may also develop a severe clotting disorder known as disseminated intravascular coagulation, which can ultimately lead to multiple organ failure and death. All midwives and obstetricians are trained to spot the signs of a placental abruption and only their swift actions, both in the diagnosis and treatment of the condition can ensure a satisfactory outcome.

As I began to talk about what had happened on Ward C3, before my transportation to the delivery suite, the look of horror and disbelief on the faces of my family and even members of staff, spoke a thousand words and I began to wonder if anything could have been done to save Thomas. My dad became very angry and vented that anger at some members of staff. He wanted answers and wanted them soon. I warned my dad that this was neither the time nor the place. At that moment my only concern was that my baby was dead, not how or why.

When my fourteen-year-old sister arrived at the hospital, it was a while before she could come into the room to see me. Like all teenagers, she thought she could face anything. What she couldn't face was the sight of her dead baby nephew. After encouragement from Stephen, she plucked up the courage to enter the room. When I saw her small pretty face, awash with tears and consumed by grief and fear, my heart went out to her. I must have looked a pretty gruesome sight. I had an intravenous drip going into my left arm, transfusing the five pints of blood which I had lost during the abruption. I also had an intravenous drip in my right hand, containing saline solution. I had a catheter bag hooked onto the side of the bed, monitoring my urine output because renal failure is a complication of a severe abruption. I was attached to a machine monitoring my blood pressure, pulse and oxygen levels and I had a canulla inserted into my main jugular vein in my neck with lots of small different coloured valves coming out of it. Basically, I was receiving high dependency post operative care. Kailey could barely find the words to speak to me and she was totally unable to find the strength to hold Thomas. However, she managed to stroke his face and tell him how much his Aunty loved him. Overnight, faced with Thomas's death, Kailey appeared to grow up from a difficult teenager into a young woman.

Soon, my thoughts turned to my brother James who had flown out to Greece with his friends for a holiday. I desperately wanted and needed him at home with us, so my mum agreed to try to contact him and tell him what had happened. It was three days before my mum managed to locate him, and a further two days before he could get a flight home. He missed out on those precious two days we spent with Thomas. Even today, he would give anything for the chance to hold him and tell him he loves him.

Chapter 4

As the sun rose, I was told that a midwife called Adrienne, who was trained to look after families like us, would arrive shortly. Adrienne was the bereavement support midwife and was there to offer us both practical and emotional support. Initially, although I did not say anything, I did not want to see her. I could hardly believe my baby was dead and although the staff were well meaning in their approach, they made me feel alien and abnormal, unworthy of being cared for by a 'normal' midwife. However, Adrienne did come to see me and ironically we did form a fantastic relationship. She has become one of my dearest friends. Without her support, I would not be the woman I am today. She is remarkable and inspirational to me in every sense.

At 9:00 am, my best friend, Ragen came. It was with her that I shared all my innermost secrets. Only she knew how much Stephen and I wanted the baby to be a boy, and she, more than anyone, knew how much I wanted this baby and how much I loved him, even before he was born. When I saw her entering the room I cried out, "It was a boy Ragen, it was a boy!"

"I know," she cried.

I asked her if she would like to hold him.

"Yes," she replied.

Ragen and I have been friends since junior school but that morning our friendship was sealed forever. When I shared my baby with her, I gave to her my most precious gift in the whole world. She was the only person outside my immediate family that I allowed to see and hold Thomas and I can still see her holding him tight to her chest and rocking him. She has since told me that her life changed forever that morning when she held Thomas in her arms. I think he changed all our lives forever and things can never be the same again.

Throughout that morning, my community midwives all came to see me. I had grown close to them during the last weeks of my pregnancy and each one of them cried with me and offered me their support. It is easy to forget that the staff are human beings, many with children of their own. These people are dedicated to the care of pregnant women and the safe arrival of their babies, so when death comes to the maternity unit, everyone is affected. I have since been told that even in the operating theatre many tears were shed when Thomas was delivered.

When a tragedy like this happens, everyone questions their clinical practice, and asks themselves if the outcome could have been different. My community midwives gave me a standard of care second to none. They are a fantastic team and I am grateful to each and every one of them. However, once I had been admitted into hospital, they had no control over the care I received. Ultimately, my life and that of my unborn baby became the responsibility of the hospital midwife, into whose care I was entrusted.

Regarding our daughter Holly, Stephen and I decided that the best thing would be for her Aunty Debbie to take her to school that morning. Stephen was to pick her up at home time to tell her what had happened. Holly excitedly told everyone at school that her mum was having the baby and soon she would be a big sister. Stephen telephoned her headteacher to tell her the news, who in turn told all her staff. That day, her Aunty Debbie and all her teachers had no choice but to listen to Holly rambling on about her new baby brother or sister, whilst knowing that the baby had died. At home time, Holly went to a local park with her dad, where he gently broke the news that she had a baby brother but he was poorly so God decided to take him to Heaven to live with him and all the angels. Holly thought for a moment, had a little cry then said, "Daddy, can I play on the swings now?"

It was hard for us as adults to understand the death of our son and the finality of it all, so how could anyone expect a six year old child to. Stephen let Holly play at the park for a while, and then brought her to the hospital. Before she came into the room, I asked for Thomas to be taken out. We decided to let Holly see pictures of her baby brother but we thought it would be too confusing and upsetting for her to see him in the flesh. To us, he was just as beautiful as ever, but his body had begun to cool down and his lips had turned a dark purple colour. Holly saw the photographs and she started to cry but she appeared more concerned with me and why I was in hospital. Even now, six years on, Holly resents the fact that she never got the chance to see and hold Thomas. At first I felt guilty for denying Holly time with her brother but I now accept that I only did what I thought was best for her at the time. In every other aspect of Thomas's death, we have tried to be very open with Holly.

Throughout the day the staff started taking Thomas out of the room, with the understanding that if at any time I wanted to see him, they would bring him back. I have since found out that it was an effort to preserve his body. He was carefully wrapped up and placed into a special cooler situated on the labour ward, which is designed especially for dead babies.

I spent the day talking to my family, I slept a little and I cried a little. My body was in total shock and this, combined with the medication and pain relief I was taking had a numbing effect on me. If I had the chance, I would do lots of things differently. With the death of a baby everyone looks back and has many regrets about how they handled the situation and I am no exception, but I have learned to live with the fact that I was too poorly and too shocked to think rationally. If I could have my time with Thomas again, I would not let go of him or let him out of my sight for one second. You do not realise how precious the time spent with your baby will become. How can you, if you have never experienced the death of your baby before. The finality of death is one of the only things that no one can change and until you are in that situation you can never contemplate the feelings of uselessness and lack of power to do anything. I recall my mum saying to me if she could rip her own heart out and give it to Thomas in an effort to give him life, she would. That was how desperate we all were to do something to bring him back to us.

It was one of the most unlikely visitors that made me realise what I had lost when Thomas died and how much everyone, not just Stephen and I, had been affected. My cousin Tina, and her husband Paul, came to visit us that evening. Tina was taken into an adjoining room to meet Thomas. Her husband stayed with me at the side of my bed. Tina's husband is a big strong man. It is unusual for him to show his emotions, but that evening when we were both alone, he took hold of my hand and just looked at me. He never said a word but I saw tears falling from his eyes. Those tears spoke a thousand words. Paul, you made me realise how much everyone loves Thomas and how he will never be forgotten and I will never forget that moment we shared.

When darkness came, I still remained in a numb and shocked state, almost like it was a dream. Stephen had initially decided to stay the night with me at the hospital. However, we were both concerned about Holly and decided that he should go home and be with her. So I found myself alone, confined to my hospital bed in the middle of the labour ward. I could hear the hustle and bustle of the busy ward and I also heard the occasional cries from newborn babies. I felt so isolated and so lonely. At that moment I wanted to be anywhere in the world, anywhere except in that hospital, surrounded by women giving birth to live, healthy babies. The midwife caring for me sat with me for as long as I wanted. She held my hand as I cried and tried to make me as comfortable as possible. In the middle of the night she asked if I wanted her to telephone a member of my family to come in and sit with me. I said no, as I thought everyone would be asleep. Not one member of my family actually slept that night. Most of them cried from nightfall to dawn, shedding more tears than they ever thought possible.

Each hour of that night felt like an eternity. I would drift off to sleep for what felt like hours, only to find when I glanced at the clock that it had been maybe ten minutes. Eventually morning came and my mum arrived. She was a welcome sight, some form of familiarity in such cold and clinical surroundings. Knowing I would probably be moved out of my room in the delivery suite that day, my mum had the task of telling me that Sarah, her friend's daughter, who we knew well and whose baby had been due the same time as Thomas, was in labour on the delivery suite. Unable to cope with the news, I just turned away. The unfairness of it all was just too much to bear.

As I was recovering well from the caesarean section, my consultant decided I could be moved to the post natal ward. Adrienne explained to me that I was to be moved to a specially designed, self contained room that offered privacy and space for bereaved parents and their families. The room was called the Snowdrop Suite. It was decided that I would take a shower in the delivery suite then make my way to the post-natal ward. Whilst walking to the shower room with my midwife, I came face to face with

Sarah and her mum. It was an awkward meeting for all of us, one which I was not prepared for. Unable to look in their direction, I just carried on walking.

After my shower, the midwife brought in a wheelchair to take me upstairs. I refused to get in, I insisted on walking. That journey was one of the hardest I have ever had to make, both emotionally and physically. As I walked onto the ward I had to pass a number of small bays, each containing four beds filled with newly delivered mothers and their babies. I walked down the ward with my head held high, looking straight ahead. Looking ahead made no difference. Images flashed before my eyes, images of all the new mums with their live and healthy babies. I could hear the sounds of the post-natal ward and almost smell the sweet smell of newborn babies. Quickly I was ushered in to the Snowdrop room. Only weeks earlier, whilst attending an ante-natal appointment, my mum and I had seen a sign for the Snowdrop Suite.

"What's the Snowdrop Suite?" my mum had asked.

"Shhh," I replied, "that's where women go when their babies have died."

And now, here I was making my way to that very room - the room for women who did not have their babies with them - the room for the women whose babies had been cruelly snatched away from them. I was grateful for the privacy that the Snowdrop room offered me. Years ago, I would have had no choice but to spend my stay in hospital among the newly delivered mothers of live babies or been banished to the gynaecology ward, as if my body had never recently delivered a baby. But that room came to feel like a prison cell to me. I felt trapped inside, unable to venture out for fear of what sights awaited me if I did.

Like a mechanical robot, I swallowed two tablets given to me. They were to stop my body producing milk. Although Thomas had died and I did not have a live baby to nourish and nurture, physically my body still needed convincing. Soon after my arrival in the Snowdrop room, Stephen had no choice but to tell me that someone who worked at the hospital had informed the local press about the events leading up to the death of Thomas. A journalist had been to both the hospital and our home to try to get information for a possible news article. I was deeply insulted and immensely hurt. This was a private time for us. It was our tragedy, not some gossip worthy of printing in a local newspaper. I now realise that the informant probably thought they were doing a good thing by exposing such a catastrophic series of events, without realising the emotional implications to Stephen and I.

Just like when I was in my room in the delivery suite, time in the Snowdrop room passed very slowly. Adrienne asked us if we wanted to see Thomas again before he was transferred to the main hospital mortuary. After some careful thought, Stephen and I both decided against it. We wanted to remember Thomas as he was and we were frightened that his physical appearance may have changed over time. Soon we also had to face the stark reality of death, when Stephen and I, had to decide what we wanted to happen to Thomas's body. For us, that was one of the hardest decisions that we, as his parents had to face. After a lengthy and heartbreaking discussion, we decided to have him cremated. On one day, Stephen went to register the stillbirth of our son and the following day he visited a local undertaker to arrange his funeral. However, whilst in hospital I tried to put our baby's funeral to the back of my mind. My only concern was getting through the day before me; I could not look to the future.

The first night I spent in the Snowdrop room, I was surprised to find I slept for a period of at least four hours. It was the first time I had had uninterrupted sleep. I awoke as the morning sun filtered through the curtains. For a split second when I woke up I felt normal, then suddenly, I remembered where I was and more importantly why. The pain in my heart was almost too much to bear and for the first time since Thomas died, I sobbed uncontrollably. I held my empty stomach and cried for my baby. That morning was the first and only time I ever contemplated ending my life. I wanted to be with my baby, I wanted to hold him, kiss him and nurse him. I thought how easy it would be to commit suicide and release myself from the utter despair I was feeling. Almost as quickly as the thought entered my mind another image drifted in, my daughter Holly and my family. How could I even think about abandoning them when they needed me so much? I still feel angry with myself for even considering such a selfish act as suicide, but at that moment in time, that was how desperate I was.

Chapter 5

I began to feel a deep dread of being on my own so I craved constant company. I became particularly protective of Stephen. If he left the hospital, even for the shortest of time, I began to panic. I imagined that something awful had happened to him. However, even in the midst of the constant stream of visitors, I still felt a sense of loneliness. I could not believe that anyone else felt the hurt of Thomas's death as much as me. How could they? They did not grow him, nurture him or feel the very essence of his spirit within them, the way I did. I now feel privileged to have been able to have such a special bond with him, but at that time I selfishly wanted someone else to feel the depth of despair and the deep hurt that I thought only I felt. However, I now realise that all my friends and family were grieving for Thomas in their own way, and I was not alone.

On Thursday the 20th July, I plucked up the courage to ask my mum about Sarah. She told me that Sarah had given birth to a baby girl. I asked if everything had gone well and I was genuinely pleased that it had. That is not to say that I did not feel a huge sense of envy. At that moment, Sarah had everything I wanted in the world, she had her baby sleeping next to her and I could not help but feel jealous.

Thursday was also the first time I discussed the events leading up to Thomas's death with someone other than my family, friends or the midwives caring for me. One of the hospital managers came to see me and I expressed my concerns about what I considered to be substandard care and what role it played in Thomas's death. It was an awkward meeting and I was still getting over the trauma of the caesarean section and the reality of Thomas's death. However, when I began to hear what I took to be patronising explanations for the questions I was firing at her; I stopped her for a moment and said, quite frankly, "I came into this hospital on Monday afternoon with a live and healthy baby and now my baby is dead, and I want to know why."

The manager appeared slightly taken aback by my approach. Until then I had remained reserved and controlled in my manner, but she did assure me that a thorough investigation would prevail, and at that point in time I believed her.

Each day I felt stronger but each night I would cry myself to sleep, listening to the cries of newborn babies coming from the ward next to my room. Although the room is situated at the end of the corridor, it is not sound proofed and the cries of babies haunted me all night. It was torturous. Instinctively I wanted to go and hold the crying baby in my arms; I wanted to soothe it and feel its soft skin against mine. I had so much love to give and wanted so much to fill my empty arms. My sense of loss was always at its worst during the night and I constantly thought about my own poor baby, all alone in the mortuary.

On Friday the 21st July, I decided to take a bath. I had a shower in my en-suite bathroom but I could not stand for long as I was still very weak. It was the first and only time I left the Snowdrop Room, other than when I first entered it and finally left for home. As Stephen and I ventured out, I felt as though everyone was watching us. I could almost hear the whispers, "There is the poor woman whose baby has died." I felt paranoid that all the mothers were clutching their babies, for fear I would snatch them, but I did not want their babies. I only wanted Thomas. In reality, if the women did clutch their babies, it would have probably been only out of sheer relief that they were not suffering like me.

Stephen helped me into the bathtub and as I sat in the water I began to cry. Obviously, as I had recently delivered a baby, I was bleeding. As I sat there, I felt I was washing away the last traces of my baby from my body. My womb was empty and I had nothing to show that a baby was ever there. My sobs echoed around the cold, clinical bathroom, as I just sat and cried. Afterwards, when the water was swirling away, down the plughole, I felt as though all our hopes and dreams were being washed away with it. We had no future, only a past.

While making my way back to my room, I caught sight of Sarah. I do not know where I found the strength from but I just had to go over and see her. As I walked towards her I could see her baby girl lying in the cot next to her bed. Sarah looked so sad when she saw me, almost guilty that she was there, enjoying the presence of her new baby. I asked Sarah how she was and I told her how beautiful her baby was. It was such a hard thing for me to do, but I am glad I did. I did not want Sarah to feel I was all bitter and twisted about the fact that Megan, as her daughter is called, was alive and Thomas wasn't. I felt only jealousy and envy towards her, not hatred or bitterness.

Finally, on Saturday the 22nd July, I was well enough to go home. I packed away all my things and accompanied by Stephen, my mum and a midwife, I left the Snowdrop Room. The room that had felt like a prison cell had also become a protective bubble and although I desperately wanted to go home, part of me wanted to stay. Before I left the room, I had one final look around and vowed never again to ever step foot in there. Now it was time to step out into the cruel world, a world which had denied me the chance to enjoy my baby boy and watch him grow up. As I walked out of the ward, into the foyer of the maternity unit, I could not help but recall the last time I had been there, a time when Thomas was safe and well in my womb. I could not believe that now I was leaving that hospital without my precious baby, I had no choice but to leave him behind.

Just as we reached the outer doors, I was met with the most heartbreaking sight imaginable. A deliriously happy couple were taking their newborn baby home. As I watched the couple carefully placing their baby into the car, the tears that I had fought so hard to keep in, just flowed from my eyes. They were taking their baby home and all I had to take home was a plastic bag containing photographs, handprints and a lock of my baby's hair. The midwife accompanying us was just as shocked as we were and kept saying over and over, "I am so sorry Shelley, this shouldn't have happened."

I told her that it was not her fault but she still could not stop crying. As we drove away and I saw the hospital fading into the distance, I kept crying, "Take me back Stephen, I need my baby."

As we neared home, through my tears, I watched people going about their business. Somehow, I expected everything to be different – the world as I knew it had changed and was never going to be the same again but people were still milling around, as if without a care in the world. At that moment I felt angry with everyone and everything around me.

Walking into our house was not as traumatic as I had feared. Although a deathly silence met us, I was grateful to be among familiar surroundings. Without saying a word, I walked through our lounge and made my way upstairs. When I opened our bedroom door, I was met by a beautifully arranged Moses basket and a chest full of lovingly washed and ironed baby clothes. I had been well prepared for our baby's birth for weeks and spent hours arranging his clothes. I sat on the bed, staring at all our baby things. Initially I did not cry but I felt a pain deep within my heart, an aching and longing to hold Thomas. I gently picked up a babygrow and held it to my chest, rocking backwards and forwards as if it contained our baby. Finally, I could not hold back any more and a long wail escaped from my lips. At that moment I needed my baby back more than ever.

Stephen came into the bedroom, but I told him I wanted to be alone. It was hours before he could persuade me to come downstairs. When I did, I sat on the sofa in a daze, while the realisation sunk in that this was my life now, and I had to try to survive without Thomas. The only trouble was, I did not know if I could.

Chapter 6

My recollection of the first week I spent at home is quite hazy. I cannot fully remember what I did with my time or how I filled my days, other than existing on auto-pilot. Although I can barely recall their presence, I know that our home was never empty. All our friends and family rallied round and tried their best to alleviate our suffering. It was during those first days at home that I began to really scrutinise the care I received on Ward C3. We were soon contacted by the Midwifery Manager who was also Head of Women's Services at the hospital where Thomas was delivered. I had requested to see my obstetric medical notes and she suggested she would come to our home and bring my medical notes with her. At that time, I was particularly interested in seeing the notes from the afternoon and evening of Monday the 17th July. I examined the CTG trace, which had been recorded at 3:00 pm. I compared it to previous recordings and although clearly, contact with Thomas's heart rate had been lost on a number of occasions, what was recorded appeared normal. So I knew that at that moment in time Thomas was not showing any obvious signs of distress, I could now concentrate on the evening. The entries made by Midwife A were self explanatory. Although badly recorded and not up to the standards set out by the Midwives Code of Conduct guidelines, they were consistent with a midwife outlining a woman in the early stages of labour. She did, however, note I had suffered some degree of blood loss, which she described as a 'heavy show'. I was mortified that she could refer to the amount of blood loss as a heavy show, when obviously the loss was enough to soak my underwear, my legs, the bedclothes and ultimately, the hospital floor.

I gave the Midwifery Manager a report I had compiled, detailing everything I could recall of my time spent on Ward C3. She assured me that an internal inquiry was about to begin and promised me that every aspect of my care would be examined in detail and appropriate action would be taken if there were any causes for concern. Maybe I was too trusting or maybe, still in shock from what had happened to us, I was just naive, but I really thought that my care would be subject to an honest and open inquiry.

With the inquiry underway, I focused my attention on the coming funeral. Each day it drew nearer, my feelings of dread and despair at our situation grew. We decided to have Thomas cremated still wearing his Winnie the Pooh outfit, as he looked so beautiful in it and we did not want him to be undressed again. We wanted to put tokens from us in Thomas's coffin, so he did not have to face his final journey alone. I cut off a lock of both mine and Holly's hair and Stephen chose his favourite Manchester United football shirt to be placed with him in his coffin. Holly also drew him a beautiful picture and I wrote a letter to him. Only I know the contents of that letter and I feel the need to keep that for myself. That first week at home, I was so desperate to have Thomas back that I often wanted to go and collect him from the mortuary. I do not remember, but one particular time, my mum recalls me begging her to help me get back to the hospital so I could get him and bring him home. It sounds irrational now, but at the time I was so desperate. I do, however, remember one particular time when I was in the company of my mum, my friend, Ragen and my cousin, Tina. I went to each one of them, asking if there was anything they could do to help me. I knew deep down that nothing could be done but I just felt compelled to ask. My mind would also play tricks on me; I imagined Thomas coming alive in the mortuary and crying for me. That was very hard for my family to cope with. I am sure they must have thought I was having some kind of nervous breakdown.

I still found myself hugging the empty baby clothes close to my heart. I would even hold one of Holly's dolls in my arms, just to try to ease the emptiness I felt. I often found myself wondering from room to room, as if I was searching for something. I now think that subconsciously my body thought it had a baby, thus I was looking for it. One day it hit me that apart from his lock of hair and his hand and footprints, which I obviously treasured, I did not have anything that Thomas had actually worn. I remembered a little green blanket that he had been wrapped in and asked my mum if she could find out what had happened to it. After several telephone calls, my mum located the blanket – it was still in the hospital mortuary. My mum went to collect it from Adrienne, armed with a clean ironed pillowcase that my Nana, forever thoughtful, had prepared to bring it home in. My Nana could not stand the thought of it being put into a plastic bag. I was upstairs when it arrived. I recall Stephen bringing it up to me, and he cried as he handed it over. It was only the second time I had seen him break down. Carefully I took the blanket out of the pillowcase and held it to my face. However, I was upset to find that the blanket smelled of the mortuary and not my sweet smelling baby. It was yet another blow to me, one that felt so unfair and cruel. Although I could not hug the blanket close to me, I still treasured it, as it had been wrapped around our baby and I could still see specks of blood on it. I have never allowed anyone other than myself to hold that blanket, not even

Stephen. People can look at it but they must not touch it. I was soon pleased to hear that my brother, James, was on his way home from Greece. He came straight to our house from the airport and the relief when I set eyes on him was immense. I showed him the pictures of his nephew and as he cried it reminded me of when we were kids. He gave me a teddy bear he had bought for Thomas and I could see the hurt and grief in his eyes. James was glad to be home but he told me how well his friends had supported him while he waited for the first available flight back to Manchester. After being told the news by my mum, he had gone into the bathroom of his hotel room. His friends knocked on the door and told him that they were his mates and if he wanted to cry, he should not feel he has to shut himself away. That evening, they also proposed a toast to baby Thomas, which really touched me. The evening James came home, he had a dream that he was holding Thomas in his arms; he held him all night. Part of me thinks that was Thomas's way of meeting his uncle and giving them the opportunity to spend time together.

Two days before the funeral, I suddenly realised I did not have a suitable outfit to wear, so I asked my Mum if she would come shopping with me. Obviously she agreed and so we went to a local shopping centre. I chose a black suit from Marks and Spencer but I felt unable to stand and queue up to pay. I left my Mum to pay and sat on a bench outside the shop. I could not believe that I was actually shopping for an outfit to wear, as we said our final goodbye to our baby. I sat in a dazed like state, barely realising when my mum returned.

I felt like a little girl again, being helped out of that shopping mall by my Mum. I still think about how my mum had to cope with me, when all the time she was grieving for her grandson. She was such a tower of strength to me and I was like a child again. I needed my Mum. I do not recall ever asking my Mum how she was, during those first few weeks. It was heartbreaking for her to have to watch her daughter hurting so much and being able to do nothing to help her, while at the same time, grieving for her grandson. I am deeply ashamed of my selfishness in not recognising her pain and suffering and only considering my own anguish. Deep down, I know my mum understands but I want to take the opportunity to tell her how much her love and support was, and still is appreciated. Mum you showed tremendous courage during those first few weeks, when I needed you, you were there for me. I only wish I had been able to offer some kind of support to you. Even today, you, more than anyone, help to keep Thomas's memory alive and I know you still miss him and grieve for him, just as much as I do. Mum, what would I do without you?

Evenings were the hardest times for Stephen and I. We would stay awake as long as possible, frightened of going to bed and being left to our own thoughts. We would watch DVDs until we fell asleep and dread those first few moments when we awoke and realised we were still living this nightmare. Initially, I was frightened of dreaming about Thomas but I was surprised when I didn't. I soon began longing to have dreams about him being alive and well. For a few hours a night, I wanted to have Thomas with me, even only in my imagination, but I didn't. It was weeks before I first dreamt about him.

Two days before Thomas's funeral, quite by chance, I showed my Nana a copy of the forms given to us by the funeral director and she noticed a vital mistake. When Stephen met with the funeral director, to arrange the funeral, he did not realise that you have to specify that you want the hearse, containing the coffin, to come to your home before the service. It was arranged that one limousine would collect us from home and we would meet the funeral cortége at the crematorium. Both Stephen and I had assumed that Thomas would be brought to our home. Imagine our horror when we realised our mistake! Quickly, further arrangements were made but I am still filled with horror at the thought of us waiting at home for Thomas, only to have him waiting at the crematorium for us.

The night before the funeral, neither Stephen nor I slept. How could we, knowing the day of our baby's funeral awaited us. The thought of the funeral filled me with deep dread and despair. I tried to concentrate on the fact that this was our last chance to say goodbye to him but I could not bear to think about the cremation process which his little body would have to endure. When morning finally came, it brought with it torrential rain. I took that to be a further insult to our suffering, but in fact, the weather just matched my mood. As our families began to arrive, I reluctantly began to get ready. I sat in the bathtub, listening to all our guests and the flowers arriving. While sitting there I made the decision that I was going to remain in control of myself to respect our baby and also to remember the day itself. I knew this day was going to be one of the worst I was ever going to have to endure and I knew I needed to muster up all the strength possible to help me through it. When I finally emerged from upstairs, I could not hold back and I started to cry, telling my mum that the rain was yet another blow.

"Shelley, that's not rain," she said, "they're angel tears, even the angels are crying with us today."

We chose to have two hymns sung at the service, 'Morning Has Broken' and 'All Things Bright and Beautiful'. Both of them reminded me of being a little girl, singing in the school choir. At times, when Thomas first died, I often yearned to be a child again, without a care in the world and many childhood memories came back to me, ones which I had forgotten until that point in time. We also chose a poem to be read out, sent to me by my Aunty Denise, called 'Nothing Loved is Ever Lost'.

When all our guests had finally arrived, I sat in our lounge with a posy of flowers on my knee, which we had chosen to be placed on Thomas's coffin. When my mum's friend, Linda arrived, she came to me, hugged me and whispered in my ear, "Be strong, Shelley," to which I replied, "You know how I am feeling, don't you?"

Linda did know how I felt, more than anyone else in the room. Many years ago, Linda lost her baby to sudden infant death syndrome. She and I were the only women in that room who had needed to prematurely say goodbye to their baby forever, knowing they would never meet again on this earth.

Finally, my dad came into the lounge and said the words I dreaded to hear. The hearse had arrived, bringing with it, our baby. When I walked out of the garden, the shock of seeing the tiny white coffin was almost too much to bear. But strangely, I also felt comforted. Here I was, within a few feet of my baby, the closest we had been for over a week. The amount of flowers we received was overwhelming; every inch of the hearse was filled with them. And in the middle of all the sweet smelling flowers was our son, confined within his tiny coffin. Numb from the reality of what lay ahead, Stephen, Holly and I climbed into the first car. As we pulled away from the kerb, I noticed some of our neighbours standing at the roadside as a sign of respect. That small gesture really touched me. When we reached the end of our road, I felt an immense urge to shout for the driver to stop; I wanted Thomas to travel in our car with us. His coffin looked so lonely in the huge hearse. I did not ask the driver to stop; I will regret that decision forever. All three of us sat in silence; I clung to Holly and pulled her tight to my chest, my silent tears falling on her small head. Holly kept asking me what was wrong. She knew it was Thomas's funeral but she did not fully understand how significant the day was. At the back of my mind, I kept telling myself to be strong, be strong for our baby. Finally we reached the crematorium and as we turned the corner I glimpsed sight of some of the midwives who had looked after us so well. I do not recall getting out of the funeral car; my first recollection is of Stephen holding his hands out, and our baby's coffin being placed into them. At last, after a week apart, Thomas had been placed into his daddy's arms for the final time. We decided beforehand that Stephen was to carry Thomas into the church. I desperately wanted to do it, but I felt it was only fair that Stephen have the privilege; after all, I had been honoured to carry Thomas for nine months. I sobbed as we walked to the altar with Thomas. As the usher gently lifted the coffin out of Stephen's arms, I kissed the name plate, kissing our baby for the last time. As we took our seats, I thought I was going to collapse. I was overwhelmed by sheer grief and sadness and an immense longing to have my baby back. Surprisingly, it was not the first time Thomas had been in that church. Only six weeks earlier, I had attended the funeral of my great aunt. Thomas had constantly kicked and wriggled all through the funeral service; as I have previously mentioned, he was such a lively baby. And so there we were, six weeks after the funeral of my aunt, in the very same church, but this time sitting in the row of pews no one ever wants to find themselves sitting in - the one at the front, the one for the immediate family of the deceased.

Thomas's funeral was a very sad but beautiful service. It was short but intimate, just as we wanted. Finally, the curtains closed and Thomas was gone forever. I recall crying out to the vicar as the curtains slowly closed, "Don't take him yet, please don't take him yet."

How I managed to leave the church without my baby, I will never know. Stephen grabbed hold of me and I was quickly ushered out. At first I tried desperately to break free. I only wanted to kiss the coffin before I left, but Stephen just carried on walking, taking me with him. When we emerged from the church we quickly climbed back into the funeral car. I pressed my face against the glass and watched as the crematorium faded into the distance. When I could see it no more, I turned and sat staring ahead, my heart aching. Suddenly I heard a little voice ask, "Mummy, what was in that white box?"

I could not find the words to answer Holly.

When we finally reached home, I sat at the kitchen table. Somebody made me a cup of tea and I sat in a state of numbness and shock. At that moment in time, I needed to block out where we had just been, I could not let my mind drift to thinking of Thomas. It was a surreal atmosphere; there was no crying or sobbing, just an awkward stillness. Everyone was guided by my lead, nobody mentioned where we had just been, or why. When I finally went upstairs to take off my suit, Stephen followed me. We sat on the bed and discussed how well everything had gone. We cried a little but we were so relieved that we had just given Thomas what we thought was a beautiful and dignified release from our world. At that moment in time, we were two proud parents, who had struggled to remain calm in the midst of such a devastating experience. I remained calm for the rest of the day, but deep down I knew that come tomorrow, the strength I had shown that day would be gone. In its place would be a state of uncontrollable grief. I was frightened, I knew what was coming, and I was right.

Chapter 7

The next morning, as I placed a rose (which I had kept from the posy on top of Thomas's coffin) into a photograph album, I suddenly remembered reading about how some people had kept bouquets and other flower arrangements by having them professionally dried. I was really upset to think that I had left the posy behind at the crematorium. I even suggested to my mum and Stephen that we should go to the crematorium and see if it was still there. Suddenly I received a telephone call from my Aunty Sharon. She told me that my Nana, who had collected all the cards off the flower arrangements for me to keep, had been unable to leave the small posy behind. She had quickly picked it up and brought it home with her. All night and all morning my Nana had been crying, feeling unable to tell me what she had done and not knowing what to do with the posy. When my aunt told me that the posy was in water, in my Nana's bathtub, I cried tears of relief and joy. We were able to collect the posy and have it professionally dried. Nana, I don't know how you do it, but you always instinctively do the right thing. I love you!

The following few days were a nightmare for Stephen and I, the pain we felt was so immense, it was uncontrollable. I began to feel a deep sense of guilt. I felt guilty that I was alive, able to breathe in the warm summer air, hear the birds singing in the trees and feel the love which surrounded me. I had barely eaten anything since Thomas had died. I was eating food which was put before me, but I found it incredibly hard to swallow anything. It was like I constantly had a lump in my throat. The following week, after Thomas's funeral, I began to use food as a way of punishing myself. If I managed to eat anything, I would make myself sick afterwards. It was not to do with my body image, or an attempt to lose weight, it was a way of punishing myself. I absolutely detest being sick, so I would eat my meals then go to the bathroom, put my head over the toilet bowl and put my fingers or my toothbrush down my throat until I was physically sick. Afterwards I felt no different, the pain was still immense, but at the time, I felt gratified that I was subjecting myself to a disgusting punishment. I would try to be as quiet as possible while I was in the bathroom, but a few times, Stephen heard me being sick. Initially, I convinced him that it was just an upset stomach but he soon began to grow increasingly suspicious. Even after only a week, I began to realise that it was becoming a habit. Images I had seen in magazines, of women who suffer from the eating disorder, bulimia, swam through my head, until one day I finally realised that I was suffering enough. Only my friend, Ragen, knew that I had begun to make myself sick and it was she that finally made me realise that I was hurting so much inside, why make myself physically ill as well.

Thomas's funeral had taken place on Friday the 28th July. The following Monday, I rang the crematorium to ask if his cremated ashes were ready for collection. It took me several attempts to pluck up enough courage to pick up the telephone and dial the number. I needed to know if he was ready to be buried, but I desperately did not want to have to face the fact that my beautiful baby, with the chubby cheeks and masses of brown hair, had been cremated. I soon heard the words I was dreading.

"He's ready to be collected."

The words swam around in my head. I quickly said goodbye and slammed the phone down. "He's ready to be collected." The words kept going around and around. They had cremated him, he was gone. I rushed upstairs and got out Thomas's photographs and his footprints. I cried and sobbed. I looked at him, my baby, who only ten days ago had been prodding and poking me, kicking me and nudging me. My son had been cremated; all I had left was a box of ash.

Monday night I had my first dream about Thomas. I dreamt I caught a bus and he was on it. For the duration of my journey, I held Thomas; I kissed him and told him how much I loved him. I sang songs to him and held him close to me, smelling his sweet smell and feeling his soft downy hair brush against my cheek. I saw his beautiful eyes lovingly looking at me and I felt his warm breath on my face as I kissed him. Suddenly, in the dream, I realised it was time for me to get off the bus. I placed Thomas on the seat next to me and got off the bus, leaving him behind. I watched the bus fade into the distance and cried and sobbed when I could see it no more. I awoke from my dream crying. Stephen tried to comfort me, but I pushed him away. At that moment in time, I wanted nobody but Thomas.

For a week after I had been discharged from hospital, I received visits from my community midwives. Although I had no baby, they still needed to check on my recovery. Every newly delivered woman has a set of notes which they keep with them, for their GP and the community midwives to keep a record of their recovery process.

These notes also contain sheets to be filled in regarding the progress of the newborn infant. On my sheets, the sections for recording the baby's progress had been crossed out, and the words RIP wrote across it in big letters. I truly understand the reasons for doing this, but those notes were a constant reminder of what I had lost. I feel there should be a set of notes available, which ask for no information about the newborn baby, in an effort to spare further heartbreak for the bereaved mother and her family. Nevertheless, I received fabulous support from my team of midwives. There was one young student midwife who had accompanied the midwives on both antenatal visits and postnatal visits to my home. I often think that she was lucky to be given the opportunity to visit a woman like me whose baby had died, to get an insight into the darker side of pregnancy and birth. In the twenty-first century, people do not realise that babies can still die during birth. Obviously technological advances mean that the rate of stillbirth and neonatal death has been dramatically reduced, but there are still many families like us, who have to face such reality and midwives need to also face this reality. At the time though, I imagined the community midwives drawing straws to decide who was to visit me that day. I assumed they felt somewhat dismayed to be visiting a woman without a live baby. I now realise that is not the case; they feel a duty to both a mother and her child and do their job accordingly.

Soon Stephen and I had the task of deciding what we wanted to do with Thomas's ashes. We finally decided that we would like to have them buried in the remembrance garden and have a tiny rosebush planted above them. The remembrance garden has a special area for babies; we chose a spot as close as possible to all the other babies and arranged for the vicar who had blessed Thomas and conducted his funeral service, to provide a small service when we buried his ashes. I wanted his ashes to be kept together in a box and I was upset to find out that the crematorium does not allow ashes to be buried in any container, they must be scattered into the earth. The day before the burial of our baby's ashes, Stephen and I went to a local garden centre to choose a rosebush. We were met by endless rows of rosebushes. Neither of us are keen gardeners and we really did not know which one to choose. We knew it needed to be a hardy bush, but we also wanted a pretty flower. We approached a woman who worked at the centre and explained that we needed to choose a rosebush under which our baby son was to be buried. I will never forget the shock on that woman's face. She must have felt I was the most heartless person to be able to stand there and say such a thing without breaking down into tears. In reality, I had been awake all night; I had cried so much that I thought I would die from a broken heart. I had spent most of the morning curled up in a foetal position on our bed, clutching a cold plastic doll tight to my chest, in an effort to try and ease the immense longing and physical pain I was feeling at the loss of my baby. I felt sad but strong at the garden centre. You see, I was doing something for my baby, I was being his mummy. I could not feed him, change him, cuddle him or sing to him, but I could choose a rosebush for him to be buried under. And it was that sentiment that kept me strong. The day before we buried Thomas, a parcel arrived from my Aunty Denise in America. She had had a star named after Thomas. A real star now twinkles in the solar system, named Thomas James William Wilkinson.

On the 4th August we buried our baby's ashes under our chosen rosebush. Just the vicar, Stephen, Holly and I were present. We wanted it to be a time for just us, a way of keeping a part of Thomas for ourselves. Any courage I had shown at Thomas's funeral was replaced by uncontrollable despair. My sobs echoed around the remembrance garden. I was oblivious to the presence of anyone other than our baby. I could not look as his ashes were exposed for the first and last time. I put my head into Stephen's chest, only feeling brave enough to look when the rosebush had been planted and the hole was covered over. We said a prayer, and then the vicar left us alone. I knelt on the grass in front of our baby's grave. I was inconsolable; I instinctively wanted to dig Thomas up there and then, as I could not stand the thought of our baby being left in the cold damp earth. I felt unable to leave him. How could I turn and walk away from our baby yet again? That morning, when I looked at that grave, feelings of anger began to emerge from within me. My baby did not deserve to be in the ground. He should have been with us, at home, warm and safe. I vowed there and then that I would do everything within my power to find some kind of justice for Thomas.

Chapter 8

The very next day, I visited the main library in the city centre. I spent hours looking for medical books concerned with obstetrics and midwifery. I wanted to find as much information as possible about placental abruption and other complications of pregnancy and delivery. I was not convinced that the problems with my blood pressure and other symptoms of pre-eclampsia had nothing to do with the abruption, as the hospital had told me. I was also not convinced that the midwife caring for me provided me with a reasonable standard of care. I selected as many books as I was allowed to take home and spent days and weeks going through them all in fine detail. I supplemented my findings with information from the internet. I surfed all the medical journal sites, accessing any relevant and up to date information. Any medical terms I did not understand, I found explanations for. My journey took me from the complete aetiology of the placenta, down to how to interpret blood results in pregnancy. I took hundreds of pages of notes; I made graphs of my blood results and blood pressure readings and I also studied my obstetric notes so much, I was almost able to recite them word for word. It soon became obvious to me that placental abruption is one of the most feared complications associated with pregnancy. However, for that very reason, all midwifery manuals and obstetric textbooks have detailed information regarding the signs and symptoms. After digesting all the information, I became convinced that I was presenting with many of the classic symptoms of abruption that a qualified and alert midwife should have picked up. The blood loss and severity of the pain should have been investigated more thoroughly. Even my obstetric history of raised blood pressure and protein urea are often associated with placental abruption. I soon realised that during my pregnancy, instead of reading endless copies of baby magazines, I should have been studying midwifery manuals, but at that time in my life I assumed that any midwife caring for me would be fully trained and competent in her practice. The trust and belief I gave to the midwife will haunt me till the day I die. Never again will I be able to completely trust the judgement of another person over my own natural instinct. I wrote a letter to the midwifery manager and included excerpts from the many medical books, outlining the symptoms I was displaying and the symptoms that should alert a midwife to a possible separation of a placenta. I received a reply stating that a full investigation was underway.

Researching placental abruption and other complications of pregnancy kept my mind busy during the day. Thomas still occupied a huge portion of my thoughts but it was at night time that I went from being a tough woman, to a grieving mother, a devastated mother, who had not only lost her baby but lost her faith in life. I began to keep a diary and wrote all my thoughts in it each night. I would write poems and letters to Thomas and it also became a release for the immense amount of emotion I felt I needed to keep secret from everyone around me. In one entry made on the 4th August, I talk of my frustration that all my friends and family were encouraging me to visit the doctor to get some anti-depressants. I realise now that they were well meaning and only had my well-being in mind, but at the time, I felt angry that people thought I could get through my grief by popping pills. I wanted to scream at them that I would only go to the doctor if he could give me my baby back. The diary is so precious to me now; it is harrowing to look back through but it also makes me realise how far I have come during the last six years. In the immediate aftermath of Thomas's death, some of the entries were so desperate; it is hard to believe that I was once the person that wrote them. On some pages I just wrote the words, 'Help me' all the way down the page; on others I would just discuss my day's events. Throughout the diary there is a strong sense of helplessness at our situation. There are a multitude of different emotions, ranging from sadness, anger, frustration and envy. Envy toward other mothers who I seemed to see constantly. It is amazing how often you glimpse sight of a pregnant woman or a mother out pushing her baby. If I saw a pram, I would feel compelled to glimpse inside. If that was not possible, I would look at the wheels to see if they looked new. If they did, I guessed a newborn baby was inside. In the early weeks, my diary describes how I would feel the presence of a dark shadow looming over me. Some days, I would feel smothered by the shadow; it felt like a huge weight bearing down on my body and soul. Other days it would be there but looming at a distance, waiting to pounce if I let my defences down and let my mind wonder.

On the 11th August, I finally decided to visit my friend, Lindsey. Lindsey had given birth to a baby boy, Ryan, just six weeks before Thomas died. It was a visit I wanted to put off, but I knew it was a milestone I had to reach, something which I needed to do, in order to try to re-build my life as best as possible. Walking into Lindsey's house, I almost had a panic attack, I was so fearful of what awaited me. I entered with trepidation and after we had greeted one another, I asked to see baby Ryan. When I saw her baby, lying in his Moses basket, I felt compelled to hold him. Lindsey handed him to me and I held him close to my chest, just as I had done with Thomas. As I rocked him, silent tears streamed down my face; inside my heart was in turmoil. Lindsey cried along with me as I held her son, wishing with all my heart that it was my baby Thomas I was holding. That evening, the dark shadow which would loom above me, was stifling. I felt smothered by its presence. My sense of despair was at its strongest. The following day, I decided to put away the Moses basket. Its presence, which initially was a comfort, had become too hard to endure. As quickly as possible, I folded all the bedclothes and dismantled the basket. I packed it all safely away and stored it in a box, ready to be put into the loft. When I was finished and I glanced at the box, I felt a huge feeling of guilt. I felt guilty and ashamed, as if packing away the box somehow signified the fact that I was beginning to forget about my baby. In reality, its presence was just too much to bear; it was heartbreaking waking up and being met by complete silence, when I wanted so desperately to be woken by the cries of my newborn waking up in his Moses basket. Stephen was surprised that I had decided to pack away the basket but he understood completely my reasons for doing it. It took me a further five days to muster up the courage to be able to pack away all our other baby things, such as the clothes, mobiles or toys we had bought.

When I finally emptied all the drawers of our baby things, I held each one in my arms before placing them into the box. I constantly found myself saying sorry to Thomas over and over, the guilt I felt was overwhelming. Before packing away the mobile we had bought for his cot, I had to wind it up and listen to the soothing music. When the musical mobile had rewound, the music stopped and in its place was a flat silence. That was when I finally began to cry. It was a poignant moment, as if the silence of the musical mobile symbolised the silence in our home. Eventually my task was finished, all our hopes and dreams for our baby and our future together as a family, was packed away into five boxes. I asked Stephen to transfer them to the loft as quickly as possible; they looked so cold and ugly waiting there, even though they contained such beautiful things.

I soon began to suffer terrible flashbacks of the night and morning of the 17th and 18th of July. A certain noise, smell or ambience would transport me right back and I would relive the events. At night, when I was alone in bed, I would go over every minute detail of the ordeal from start to finish. I felt very angry at the obvious delay in recognising I was having a placental abruption and the appalling way I was treated by Midwife A. I desperately wanted someone from the hospital concerned to recognise what I saw to be obvious neglect. I only wanted that and maybe an apology from Midwife A. We are only human and I know people can make mistakes. I just wanted Midwife A to acknowledge my grief at the death of Thomas and maybe some reassurance that something like this would never happen again. Friends and family told me that the hospital would back their midwife and cover up any potential concerns but I believed that they would be very honest and open. After all we had lost our son. Thomas had died. His most precious thing in the whole world had been taken away from him, his life.

Chapter 9

On 25th August, the morning post brought with it what we had been waiting for. It was the first report compiled by the inquiry team. I ran upstairs to my bedroom, where Stephen was. Slowly, with Stephen sat beside me, I opened the letter and began to read it. The shock and disbelief I felt when I scanned the pages will stay with me forever. What was written on those pages was an insult to my intelligence and my integrity but most of all, it was an insult to our baby. The report is too long to discuss in detail, but I will give an outline of what it contained. We were offered tokens of sympathy and throughout the report I was given apologies for 'feeling that I was left alone, in pain.' I was offered an apology for 'feeling that the midwife did not listen to me when I told her I was frightened for the safety of my baby.' I was offered an apology for 'feeling that the care I received was substandard,' and so on. Each one of the concerns I had raised was dismissed as my own misinterpretation of events. The report suggested that I was initially in the early stages of labour and I had suffered the abruption only when being transferred to the delivery suite. My version of events and that of Midwife A were also remarkably different. Midwife A did not recall my telling her I was suffering constant pain. She suggested that I did not lose a lot of blood. She also suggested that I gave no inclination that I was at all distressed. Rather, she just assumed I was getting myself 'worked up.' She even denied that I asked to be taken to the delivery suite on the bed or that I slipped on the blood on the floor, both of which Stephen and I remember clearly. They tried to keep me quiet by offering me sympathy and token apologies, while never actually admitting that any of my concerns were valid or even bore some truth.

I became determined to fight for some kind of justice for our baby, and any other baby born in that hospital, under the care of that midwife. That said, I was still thrust into a week of blackness and despair and feelings of frustration with a huge sense of grief as a direct result of the attitude of the hospital management team. After considering my options I decided I needed to do two things. Firstly, I felt the need to speak with my consultant, as I felt he was not aware of the circumstances leading up to the abruption. Secondly, I felt I needed to write to the Head of Women's Services, outlining my concerns about the findings of the initial inquiry. I sent both letters and I received an appointment to attend a meeting with my consultant on the 30th August. In the meantime, Stephen and I needed to go back to the registry office so we could collect Thomas's stillbirth certificate. I would have liked to have a 'birth' certificate as I feel that Thomas deserves recognition that he existed, but as the law stands, we were issued with a 'stillbirth' certificate. I felt insulted, as if it implied that my baby had never existed. If he had been born alive and lived for seconds, we would have been issued with a birth certificate and a death certificate, but in the eyes of the government, I assumed that my baby's presence was not important. I wanted to challenge the person who made such decisions and ask then to tell me how they could dismiss Thomas's being, when I had felt him move for months and even seen him moving on ultrasound scans. We left the registry office with a blue stillbirth certificate and a broken heart.

In the lead up to our meeting with my consultant, I began to feel my head would explode with all the information I had gathered. I began to question whether our quest for the truth and some form of justice for Thomas was beginning to have an effect on my grieving process. The only time I was able to escape the deep pain I felt within my heart, was when I had my head in a medical book. Obstetric terminology would swim through my mind. I read so many medical books and journals that Thomas almost became depersonalised to me. I began to inadvertently think of him as a foetus and the way he died as a 'foetal death in utero', which in laymen's terms means the baby has died in the womb, before birth. One day, whilst searching a well known medical journal in my local library, it suddenly hit me. Thomas was not a foetus, he was not a foetal death in utero; he was my baby, my little boy. The shock of that realisation hit me like a ton of bricks. I threw down the journal I was reading and ran out of the library. I drove to the crematorium and sat on the grass in front of my baby's grave. I talked to him, telling him how much we loved him and were all missing him. Whilst I sat there I almost made my mind up to forget all about the inquiry and just try to re-build our lives as best as possible. I felt torn; I felt the whole inquiry was a huge cover up. I trusted no one who worked at the hospital, well no one except Adrienne, the bereavement support midwife, who I had begun to see on a regular basis. The inquiry report told such convincing lies that even I began to question my own sanity. I knew that I had definitely experienced what I reported to the hospital. If they were saying such events did not happen, then I could only assume that either I was going mad or the report was full of lies.

In the following weeks I began to push Stephen away from me. I felt stifled by the attention I was receiving from him and everyone around me. But strangely, I also felt the need to constantly talk about Thomas and I became convinced that everyone was getting fed up with my constant ramblings. We were a typical working class family and we turned to each other in times of crisis, it was not the norm for us to turn to outside help. But, over the following months, I found it hard to talk to my family, even Stephen, about how I felt. How could I inflict my sorrow onto them when they themselves were so consumed by grief?

My sessions with Adrienne were an opportunity to off-load all my emotional anxiety and grief, especially concerning the neglect I felt contributed to Thomas's death. Unlike my family, she was not emotionally involved and although she showed me immense compassion at the death of Thomas, she was able to remain neutral and let me ramble on to my heart's content. It was only during my meetings with Adrienne that I felt totally able to open up and talk about my feelings. It was she who finally made me realise that I was not going mad, which I had increasingly begun to think; I was just a mother who was going through a process of grieving for her baby. Adrienne was more than happy to visit our home to see me, but for some reason I felt compelled to visit her in her counselling suite which is actually situated on Ward C3, in the maternity unit. I always felt a huge sense of sadness and a yearning to have my baby back whenever I ventured on to the unit, but that was where most of our meetings took place. For a long time, I was never able to look at Room 2 on the ward as that was the room where I initially suffered the abruption, and in my opinion, the place where Thomas died, but one day I asked Adrienne if she would take me into it. I walked into the room and sat on the hospital bed. Images of the last time I had been there flashed through my mind. I saw the clock on the wall, where on the night of 17th July I had watched the minutes ticking by, while trying to muster up enough strength to try to alert the midwife. I saw the nurse alarm call, which was still situated in a holder high on the wall beside the bed, and I recalled my efforts to try to reach it without moving off the bed. I saw the huge window where I had watched the last of the summer sun's rays fade into darkness and I glanced at the floor, which only weeks earlier had been covered in my own blood, as it flowed from my womb. As quickly as these images came to me, they were gone and I soon realised that it was just a room, it was not a torture chamber as I had recalled, just a simple room.

On 5th August, Stephen and I met with my consultant. I must stress at this point that this was a different consultant I had booked in with for the duration of my pregnancy with Thomas. It was the consultant who had been on call the evening of 17th July. It was he who delivered Thomas and saved my life in the process. My original consultant never even bothered to visit me for the duration of my stay in hospital, even to offer her condolences and in all honesty I preferred my new consultant and his style of clinical practice immensely. As organised as ever, I had decided beforehand what I wanted to discuss at the meeting and in what order. We received what we took to be honest answers to our queries. Basically, the consultant believed that the abruption happened just prior to my being removed to the delivery suite. Obviously he and I had no contact that evening until Thomas was already dead and the abruption had definitely occurred. He could only make assumptions based on his clinical findings when they eventually opened my uterus to deliver Thomas. What he found was that most of the placenta had become detached from the uterine wall, with only a very small amount of placental tissue still intact. In his opinion, the abruption I suffered was so massive and so severe that if it had occurred when I suggested and I had been bleeding from a much earlier point in the evening, then the blood loss would have resulted in almost a total body shut down or death. But he did agree that this was only an opinion relating to his experience and all situations are different. Without ever having any contact with me prior to my transferral to the delivery suite, he was unable to give us a definitive answer. I will always insist that the pain and blood loss I experienced between the hours of 9:30 and 11:00 did indicate that the placenta had begun to detach from the wall of my uterus. It was a constant and agonising pain, and definitely too much blood to be regarded as 'a show', which is a plug of mucus which closes off the entrance to the womb in pregnancy. I soon began to realise that our plight for any form of justice for the death of our son could only be decided on the testament of two people, myself and Midwife A. I felt deflated and helpless; I began to fear we were fighting a losing battle, one that was becoming ever more stressful.

The days following the meeting with the consultant were very hard, as if I had convinced myself that he would provide us with the answers to all our concerns and ultimately make things better. In reality, he could not offer us a full explanation for what occurred, nor could he make us feel any better as he could not give us what we wanted more than anything, our baby back!

Later that week, I received a letter from the head of women's services inviting us to attend a meeting with her and the NHS Trust's Clinical Risk Manager. Under pressure, the Trust had decided to appoint a panel in order to ascertain if a 'Serious Untoward Incident' had taken place and also to try to decide what action, if any, would be taken against the Trust or the midwife in question. A meeting was arranged for 18th September. In the meantime, I prepared myself for the beginning of September, when Stephen planned to go back to work,

Holly started back at school and I returned to university for the second year of my undergraduate course. I felt I needed to get back to my studies as I was frightened about what I would do with my time without Stephen or Holly being around during the day. On the 1st September, Stephen's alarm went off at 6:30 am. That morning as Stephen got ready for work, it was a surreal atmosphere, almost like Thomas's birth and death had been a dream. Even at that point, I still found the whole situation hard to believe. Full term babies do not die! Was I ever pregnant in the first place? On 4th September, I dressed Holly in her new school uniform and we set off for the drive to school. I had been dreading this moment for a long time. It should have been such a joyous occasion, with Holly and I showing off our new baby. Instead we walked hand in hand together through the school gates, the absence of a new pram evident for everyone to see. At my request, my friend, Ragen, had done an excellent job in informing as many mums as possible about what had happened to Thomas. The mums I knew well came up to me and offered their condolences. The ones I knew less, tended to shy away, unable to find the words to convey how sorry they were and also not wanting to intrude. I finally made it to the sanctuary of Holly's classroom but when I entered, one of the mums, obviously seeing the absence of my pregnant stomach, came rushing over. "Well?" she asked, "What did you have? Was it a boy or a girl?"

I just knew that it was going to happen; I knew someone was going to say those words to me but they still came as a shock.

"I had a boy," I replied, "but he has died."

Any amount of shock I felt at that moment was completely engulfed by the look of pure horror and embarrassment on that poor woman's face. She profusely apologised, but I understood that it was a simple mistake;

she did not mean to cause me any pain. Having said that, I literally ran out of the classroom and only felt safe when I was back in my car. I sat and cried for a few moments then drove home, relieved that I had overcome yet another hurdle.

With Holly back at school and Stephen back at work, I spent a lot of time at the crematorium. I would go three or four times a week, sometimes twice in one day. Thomas has a small plot into which his rosebush is planted. I bought small vases so I could arrange flowers around the bush. We placed a teddy bear on the grave and I would often leave poems and letters to Thomas. I would sit on the grass in front of his grave and talk to him. Initially, I poured out all the guilt I felt that I let him die and did not insist that the midwife fetch a doctor to assess my situation. I would tell him how sorry I was. I do not think I ever really truly believed that Thomas could hear me, but I just felt compelled to talk to him. On windy days I would feel compelled to go to his grave, just in case his pots of flowers or his teddy bear had blown over. I bought a small gardening kit which contained a miniature trowel, spade and a small set of gardening scissors. Buying the set brought me so much pain, I could not help but think that I should be buying toys and new clothes for our baby, not a gardening set to tend to his grave.

Chapter 10

My diary extract for 5th September pays specific attention to the fact that Stephen and I both agreed that the nightmare of losing Thomas appeared to be getting worse. I write how frightened I feel that I can see no end to the raw burning pain I feel at the absence of Thomas. I feel despair that I have to live the rest of my life without him, enduring such horrific pain. I ask myself will it all become too much to bear. Will I eventually crumble? The following is a letter and poem, taken from my personal diary, written by myself, on that very same day:

Dear baby Thomas,

I know I have said to you numerous times that I will see this inquiry to the end but sometimes I feel that in order to really grieve for you, I have to let go of it. I am up against a very powerful organisation; the NHS will not admit any incompetence on behalf of their midwife, without a fight. I do not feel strong enough to carry on with the inquiry. I will not even attempt to ask you to forgive me, as I cannot forgive myself.

Thomas, I love you so much. If there was anything I could do to bring you back home, I would.

I miss you, my baby.

Love your heartbroken mummy xxx

Help Me
I feel like a candle and someone's blown out my light,
I feel even in daytime, the darkness of the night,
Inside my soul is lonely,
My mind is constantly in a scream,
Help me, save me, rouse me,
Wake me from this painful dream,
Give me back my baby,
And my torment will come to an end,
Give me back my baby,
And my shattered heart will mend.

Surprisingly, only a few days later, the strength to keep going finally came back to me. I realised that what was holding me back from carrying on with the inquiry was the thought of living the rest of my life, knowing that Thomas could have been saved if a different midwife had cared for us, and he died from neglect or because a midwife had become complacent in her job. But whatever the outcome, I needed to know, I would just have to face the fallout, if and when it came.

If you have noticed that I have barely mentioned my daughter, Holly, or my partner, Stephen; that is because for the first months after Thomas's death, I was locked in my own world. I am ashamed to admit it, but I can only vaguely remember the presence of Holly, Stephen or any other members of my family. I know they all played a huge part in my grieving process but I was so wrapped up in the death of Thomas and the ensuing inquiry that they seemed to just linger in the background. When I look back and remember how I pushed everyone, including Holly away from me, I am surprised because all through my pregnancy, I vividly recall worrying that I would never be able to love any child the way I love Holly. She was, and still is, the centre of my world and I thought I would never be able to love another human being the way I love her. So with reflection, it is hard for me to realise how I managed to exist in my own world. Eventually with time, I allowed both Holly and Stephen to become close to me again. It was not something that happened overnight; my relationship with them just slowly got back to normal. My relationship with Stephen has grown stronger since Thomas died. From the moment we met, fifteen years ago, I just knew we would be together forever but the death of a child can sometimes have devastating effects on the relationship of the parents, we were lucky. Although we grieved in totally different ways, we were patient with each other. My only grievance with Stephen was that I wanted him to express how he was really feeling, but that is something Stephen will never do; it is not in his nature.

One area we did slightly disagree with was the fact that I immediately wanted another baby. This is not unusual; many women who experience a stillbirth or a neonatal death feel an overwhelming longing for another baby. I discussed my feelings with Stephen but he was adamant that we needed to wait. Again, feeling unable to embark on another pregnancy is not unusual for men. I initially felt we were pulling in two separate directions. Eventually, Stephen opened up to me and told me his reason for being reluctant to try for another baby – he was frightened that he could lose me, as well as another subsequent baby. I was so wrapped up in my own grief that I failed to realise that on the evening of 17th July, Stephen stood and watched helplessly as I slipped further and further away from him, right before his eyes. Most men feel the need to protect their family, something that he was simply unable to do. Not only did his son die that evening, but he nearly lost me too, the woman he had shared his life with for nine years, and the mother of his daughter. For him, the risks of another pregnancy were at that time, just too much to bear. I also discussed having another baby with Adrienne. After many lengthy counselling sessions, I realised that I needed time to grieve for Thomas and allow him to take his place within our family. Stephen and I decided that we would wait a year and then embark on another pregnancy. However, secretly every month I hoped my period would be late. Some months I became convinced that I could feel a baby moving in my womb. One time I even convinced myself I was pregnant. I had a pregnancy test at my local chemist. The result was negative - I was devastated.

Chapter 11

When the day came to meet with the Head of Women's Services and the Clinical Risk Manager, I again prepared, in minute detail, the areas of my care I wanted to focus upon. If I am honest, I was initially wary and untrusting of both the women we were meeting. My trust regarding the Head of Women's Services had been previously shattered after receiving the hospital's initial report into the death of Thomas and we had never before met the Clinical Risk Manager. I was polite as usual but also very defensive as I went through the events leading up to my transferral to the delivery suite. It was a strained meeting, with the Clinical Risk Manager listening while the Midwifery Manager and I went through each aspect of my care. At the end of the meeting, I felt that we were nowhere nearer solving any of the problems highlighted, which I found very frustrating. After obtaining my medical records and all the relevant statements made by everyone involved with the case, the Clinical Risk Manager, who I will refer to as Gill, prepared a report to be examined at by the Serious Untoward Incident panel. I received a copy of the report and in my opinion, it was an unbiased and fair account of the events. Although I still remained wary, for the first time in months, I felt able to lay some trust in someone employed by the NHS and at that time, that was particularly important to me.

On the 7th August and the 30th August, the panel met to discuss my case. I have always felt we were under-represented at the meeting. I was not allowed to attend and the panel consisted of various lay persons, and a medical doctor who was not an obstetrician. The only person on the panel with any obstetric experience was my consultant and I already knew his opinion regarding the case. However, I remained optimistic.

Some weeks later, I received a telephone call from Gill. She was calling to inform me that I would soon be receiving the findings of the review panel. When we received the letter, we were devastated to read that the panel had concluded that a 'serious untoward incident' had not taken place. Attitudinal issues were identified, regarding the midwife involved and the panel agreed that I was not listened to during my time in her care. Again, they made reference to the discrepancies between my version of events and those of the midwife and it was clearly obvious that they had found it hard to ascertain if a delay in the diagnosis of my condition had occurred. I felt hurt and let down by the inquiry. It was hard to comprehend what the NHS would consider to be a serious incident. How could I visit the grave of my child and try to come to terms with the fact that no one was going to be held responsible for the consequences of what happened. For Stephen and I, it was never about revenge or compensation; it was about recognition of our loss and protection for future pregnant women and their unborn babies.

What follows is an extract from my personal diary, dated 9th October, 2000

Dear Thomas,

Again, our attempts to make the hospital recognise and admit there were problems with our care, have resulted in nothing. I do not know how far I can take this as our options are narrowing. We could hire a solicitor but that is a route I never want to go down. Thomas, I have a constant lump in my throat. I feel that I am going to burst into tears any minute. My heart is hurting so much tonight. Nobody understands how painful this is for me. I feel overwhelmed by sadness and my need to have you with me. How can I live without you?

Chapter 12

The 10th October started out just another normal day. I had an appointment with Adrienne in her counselling room on Ward C3. I made my way out of the hospital lift and met Adrienne at the ward doors. As usual, we began to make our way to her room. Suddenly, walking toward me I glimpsed sight of the midwife. I initially thought I was mistaken, however I soon realised it was definitely her. For the previous months, I had been very vocal about what I would do if I ever met up with her and as you can imagine I thought when we did finally meet again, I would confront her about what happened. Instead of a confrontation, we walked past one another. I was so shocked. It was so unexpected, and the midwife looked just as shocked as I was. Unbeknown to Adrienne, who always went to great lengths to ensure I never came face to face with the midwife, Ward C3 was understaffed and she had been sent from the post-natal ward to help out. Neither Adrienne nor I said a word to one another until we reached her room and she asked me if I realised who I had just walked past. It was strange sitting in Adrienne's room, knowing the woman who had made a huge contribution to the pain and suffering my family and I had endured for the past three months, was working only metres away from me. My stomach was doing summersaults, images of the previous time I had met that woman, as I lay in excruciating pain, flashed before my mind. Even today, I find it hard to believe that I sat in Adrienne's room for an hour, knowing that woman was nearby, without running to her and confronting her about what had happened. For days, even weeks after that chance meeting, I felt an enormous amount of shame and guilt. I felt that I had let Thomas down in some way for not approaching the midwife.

Today, I feel proud that I did not embarrass myself and make a scene in the maternity unit. I know most people would believe that I was justified in any attempt to confront the midwife, but from the outset of the inquiry, I remained dignified in my approach to both the midwife herself and the maternity unit. That, I believe, is a valuable reflection of the person I was then and still am today.

Soon, I received a telephone call from Gill, the Trust's Clinical Risk Manager. I was told that as a result of the inquiry panel meeting, it had been decided that an independent obstetrician was to look into my case and give his professional opinion. I soon found out that the NHS were footing the cost of this and it was a highly unusual route for them to go down in a non-medical litigation case. I was informed that as a matter of protocol, the Trust was to hand my case to their legal team, so they were ready to act if the expert opinion fell in our favour. At that point, I decided that I needed to contact some form of legal representation myself. If the Trust felt it was necessary, then I decided to go by their lead. After researching various legal practices which had a good reputation for clinical negligence cases, we contacted a well respected firm of solicitors. From the start they were confident that they could secure some form of compensation for the death of Thomas and the psychological implications that had on me. However, they did suggest that the very nature of placental abruption, and its often devastating affect, gave the Trust some form of strength to its case. Nevertheless, we were confident that the independent obstetrician would agree there were failings in our care and we would not have to go down the litigation route.

After the recent internal inquiry, the midwife was placed on supervisory practice for a number of months. Like a student midwife, she was unable to practice alone and was required to meet various standards before she was allowed to practice as a fully fledged midwife again. Clearly, Stephen and I took that to be some form of recognition of her failings. However, as she had never acknowledged the full extent regarding the incompetence of the care she gave Thomas and I, and the fact that in our view she lied about the events that happened on Ward C3, we still felt the need to pursue our endeavour to find out how much her actions contributed to Thomas's death. In our opinion, how can anyone change if they cannot admit there were problems in the first place?

Chapter 13

Summer soon gave way to autumn, a season I had always loved in the past. The leaves on the trees still shone in their brilliant hues of red, yellow, orange and gold, a sight which had been so beautiful to me in the past. However, this year I could not look at such beauty without enduring feelings of overwhelming grief and guilt. I felt guilty that I was alive and able to enjoy life; that I could see the autumn leaves and feel the cool wind upon my face. I truly believed that I would never be completely happy and at peace with myself ever again. Autumn also brought with it rain and showers. The grass in front of Thomas's grave became waterlogged and muddy which spoilt the time I spent at his grave and that was all I had left. Each time I visited him I would stay back until Stephen and whoever else had come with us, had left to go to the car. From the first day his ashes were laid to rest in his grave, until this very day, I always say sorry to him before I leave. I tell him I am so sorry that I could not save him and I let the midwife convince me everything was okay. I say sorry that he is in the ground and I can go home. I say sorry that I am alive and he is not. If Stephen and my mum often wonder why I always stay behind on my own for a few minutes, they now know the reason. Apologising to Thomas does not make me feel any better; it does not ease my feelings of failure and guilt, but I just feel compelled to say sorry every time I leave him.

Winter came and as Christmas drew near I began to feel overwhelming sadness. We could just about cope with our grief everyday but at special times such as Christmas, the loss of a child would be so hard to bear. I knew I needed to make Christmas special for our daughter Holly, but inside the pain I felt was at some times almost unbearable. I always loved putting up our Christmas tree. Holly and I would play Christmas carols as we decorated the tree and our house. We tried so hard that year to try to make it as normal as possible but it was difficult. Each Christmas is hard to bear but that first one was definitely the worst. On Christmas morning I watched Holly open all her gifts and found it hard not to cry. After breakfast we headed for the crematorium. Secretly I wrapped a present for Thomas, a new teddy bear, and rushed to the grave to put it there. We told Holly that Father Christmas had not forgotten Thomas and asked her if she would like to open his gift. As I sat at his grave it began to snow. Not heavy, just a small flurry that lasted about five minutes. Whilst sitting there watching, a small frosting of snow covered his rose bush and I felt happy and contented. However, when it was time to leave it was dreadful. I thought about our warm cosy house and the fact that in a few hours we would be sitting around the table, eating turkey and I felt physically sick. The sickness lasted all day; I was unable to swallow even one tiny morsel of my Christmas dinner. That evening as I lay in bed, I thought about the midwife. I wondered if she thought about my poor baby lying in his grave as she watched her children opening their presents. I hoped she felt wracked with guilt.

In January we arranged a date to meet with the independent obstetrician who was to review our case. On a cold, damp January morning we set out to meet with him. I felt nervous inside, like this was our last chance to secure some form of justice for Thomas. During the journey we passed the crematorium. I glanced over to where our baby lay buried and hoped that finally someone would agree that Thomas had not been given a fair chance of living.

The obstetrician was an older and very experienced doctor who now practiced independently of the NHS. His consulting rooms were furnished with ageing but obviously expensive furniture. From the moment we entered, I felt totally out of place but when we met the obstetrician, I warmed to him immediately. He had in front of him my medical notes and various witness statements taken from key members of the medical staff who had come into contact with me prior to, and after the placental abruption. I started from the beginning and recalled everything I could remember from the afternoon and evening of Monday July the 17th. I was asked many questions and answered them all. We discussed placental abruption and the effect it can have on an unborn child and we also discussed the feasible time needed to perform an emergency caesarean in the hope of delivering a live and physically healthy baby.

I recalled how I had known that something was wrong but that the midwife caring for me convinced me in her uncaring way that I was getting worked up. He was particularly interested in the nature and intensity of the pain I was suffering. The consultation lasted around two hours. At the end we were given the opportunity to ask questions. We asked many but I finally plucked up the courage to ask how Thomas died and if he would have been aware of any pain and suffering. During the course of my research, I have read that as babies become deprived of oxygen, they begin to rapidly move about. I had suffered nightmares of my baby thrashing around in my womb, as he slowly suffocated. The obstetrician told us that as the placenta detached from my uterine wall, Thomas's oxygen levels would have slowly decreased until he slipped into unconsciousness. Death would have followed without Thomas being aware of anything. The obstetrician likened it to having a general anaesthetic and a patient never waking up. In fact he suggested that given the choice it was the way he would like to go when his time was up. On hearing this news, it was the only time I cried during our meeting but they were tears of relief, relief that Thomas did not suffer as I had so often imagined. I was now reassured that the last sound Thomas would have heard as he slipped into unconsciousness and finally died, was the sound of my beating heart - a heart that was filled with so much love and affection for him. At least when Thomas left our world, he went peacefully and was not alone - he was inside his mummy.

Whilst battling with the stress of losing Thomas and the ensuing inquiry, I also threw myself into my university studies. A small selection of my tutors knew what had happened to me but I never asked for special provision to be made. I knew if I did, I would receive all the help I needed. However, it was good to go to university and just feel normal. When I was there, I was just Shelley the student, not Shelley the grieving mother, and it was refreshing to be able to try to carry on as usual. I am not saying that it was not difficult for me. When I was working on an assignment and had deadlines to meet, it was hard to stay focused. I just wanted to use any spare time to conduct more research, not write essays, but I battled through and successfully completed my second year. When I sat my end of year exams it was hard not to think about the last time I sat in the very same hall when I was seven months pregnant with Thomas. At the time I felt special. I was the only person in the room who had another person with them. He wriggled and kicked and prodded throughout each three hour exam but I relished the fact that he was there with me, sharing my anguish. Of course during my second year exams, I was totally alone and I felt totally alone. Nevertheless, I passed all my exams with flying colours. Convinced I must have failed, I asked my friend Peter to collect my results from the university. I cried tears of joy when he telephoned to say I had passed. Inside I was saying over and over, "I did it Thomas. I did it for you!" I endeavoured to finish my degree and dedicate it to my baby son, who had come into our lives so unexpectedly and who left us so needlessly. In my darkest hour, I would not let the stress of studying beat me. Any weakness on my part would have been a huge let-down to Thomas.

By referring to my diary, I am aware that during the month of January, I began to question the reasons that Thomas was taken from us. We are not a religious family but I felt a strong need to try to find a meaning for his death. I began to have feelings that I was chosen in some way, chosen to conceive Thomas but was never destined to keep him. With hindsight, I believe that I was trying to cling to the fact that if I believed in an afterlife, I would eventually be united with Thomas again. I suppose the thought of never, ever seeing him again was just too much to bear. Today, six years on, I realise and most importantly can accept that Thomas and I will never meet again. It still upsets me to admit this to myself, that all I have left of Thomas are the memories of the short time we spent together. Even the emptiness that I felt in the early months has faded. At every family gathering I feel the loss of his presence but I am now able to accept that Thomas has a place in our family; his place is not an empty void but is filled with the memory of him. Nothing and no-one can take the memories away from me. I accept that they will become a little blurred with time but I will remember him forever.

Chapter 14

On the 20th January, I received a telephone call from the then chief executive of my local NHS Trust. She called to tell me that they had received a copy of the independent review. That afternoon she was to share the report with the people involved and also send a copy to me. I did not enquire about the findings of the report; I merely waited in anticipation for my copy. The very next day, the report came. The report detailed the obstetric history of both my pregnancies but it mainly focused on the evening of 17th July, 2000. References were made to the entries made by the midwife in my medical notes along with my testimony of events and that of the midwife. The midwife maintained that I was in early labour, that I had experienced what she described as a 'heavy show' and that I specifically told her the pain 'came and went'. By her own admission the midwife concluded that I 'was getting myself worked up'. That I believe, was the reason she gave for not helping me when I repeatedly told her I was starting to panic, as I felt that something was wrong. In their statements, both she and the midwife who came to collect me from the delivery suite denied that I was in a distressed state or that I wanted to be left on the bed when I was transferred to the delivery suite. They also did not see my feet slipping in my blood, which was strange as they were both helping me walk across the floor when it happened. The obstetrician suggested that if this case was to go to court, the judge would have the unenviable task of trying to decipher who was telling the truth. He did admit that I was an obviously intelligent woman and I provided a believable version of events. He concluded by saying that if my account was correct, then the care provided to me by the midwife involved was not of an acceptable standard but he further suggested that even by the midwife's own account, her care fell short of what is acceptable. He made reference to the fact that Thomas's heart rate should have been listened to when the blood loss or as she noted 'heavy show' was observed and again after she had performed an internal examination. Regarding the timing of the abruption, and if a different approach to the management of the events that evening would have saved Thomas, he suggested that the abruption most probably started around 21:00 hours and by 22:00, the pain was so severe that a major bleed had already occurred. He was doubtful due to the time needed to perform even an emergency caesarean that Thomas would have survived. At best, he claimed that our baby may have been born very severely mentally and physically brain damaged, but even the odds on that were extremely low. It was noted that both midwives' testimony stating that I was not in a distressed state at 22:30 hours could not be true, as by that time I had suffered a major bleed and was showing obvious signs of hypovolaemic shock.

At last Stephen and I felt that this was some recognition of the failing in our care. I understood the reality of the time needed from when a decision to perform an emergency caesarean is taken, to the actual delivery of the baby. This does not happen within minutes like in the movies, but I was left with the feeling that had the midwife listened to Thomas's heart rate, he may have been showing signs of distress. If I had received optimal care and Thomas had still died, then I would be able to accept that nothing could have been done to save him. However, the care I received leaves me no option but to always fear that in the care of a different midwife, Thomas may have stood a chance of survival. That is something I have to live with for the rest of my life.

Accompanying the report was a letter from the chief executive. Within the letter, the main issues arising from the independent report were highlighted and responses given. It was agreed that the assessment of Thomas's well-being fell short of an acceptable standard. The midwife had agreed that she should have listened to the foetal heart when blood loss had been observed and she could give us no explanation as to why she hadn't. In response to the attitudinal issues highlighted, the Trust suggested that during her period of supervisory practice, the midwife had worked hard to improve her clinical practice and her attitude toward patients and their families. We were informed that she had achieved all the required standards and as such was able to regain her midwifery status. We were offered a formal apology for being let down by the Trust and the consequences of that night. It came as a huge relief to Stephen and I. However, I was left with the dilemma of deciding if a few weeks supervisory practice and an apology from the Trust justified what our family, especially Thomas, had suffered. Part of my conscience was telling me to close the chapter of the book and try to rebuild our lives.

After further contact with our solicitor it became apparent that they would not be able to hold the midwife personally accountable for her actions. As I have mentioned previously, a placental abruption is a devastating occurrence with often devastating consequences. It would be virtually impossible to force the Trust to admit liability. Again, we were informed that it would be likely we could claim some form of compensation for the trauma and suffering I had been subjected to, but without the hope of any action taken directly against the midwife concerned, we declined to take our case any further. Many relations and friends urged us to seek financial compensation; they suggested we deserved some form of financial security after everything we had been through. At the time we could not contemplate the thought of spending any money given to us to compensate the death of our son. As I have previously explained, our fight was never, ever about money.

In June, 2001, a year after Thomas died, we decided it was time to try for another baby. I found out I was pregnant with my third baby a week after Thomas's first birthday. From the onset, my pregnancy was classed as high risk. I was never in any doubt that I would book into the same hospital. On the whole, the care I received was good and after Thomas died, it was excellent. I booked in with the obstetrician who had delivered Thomas. I will never forget what he said to me on my first visit to him. He said that although he could not guarantee that nothing would go wrong this time, he would use everything within his knowledge and power to ensure that I delivered a live and healthy baby. That was exactly what I wanted to hear. If he had claimed that nothing would go wrong, I would have lost faith in him. Almost all pregnancies result in a happy ending but as I now know, every pregnancy has the potential to have problems. I hope when he reads this, which I am sure he will, my obstetrician realises how hard it was for me to place my trust in another human being and prides himself in being the only person I could have entrusted the life of my unborn baby to. Thank you Mr. W.

The pregnancy was at times fraught with anguish and anxiety. I knew that the obstetric care I was receiving was excellent but I also knew that if I suffered another placental abruption, it would be a race against time to save our baby. I was also wracked with guilt. As I felt our child growing within me, I was reminded of Thomas and how it felt to carry him. At times, although I loved our new baby immensely, I felt he was in someway stealing my love and attention away from Thomas. We were told when I had my eighteen week anomaly scan that our baby was a boy. I remember Stephen just clutching my hand tightly as we were told the news. Although I wanted another little boy, I was frightened that when he was born, he would be the image of his brother, Thomas. Somehow I battled through the pregnancy. I was subjected to intense obstetric care but I was willing to accept any form of reassurance that the baby growing inside me was healthy, and more importantly, alive.

On 13th February, 2002, when I had reached thirty-five weeks and five days gestation, the result of my weekly examination at the hospital indicated that the baby was not as happy in my womb, as he had been the previous week. A Doppler scan had revealed that the blood flow from the placenta to the baby, which carried oxygenated blood and nutrients, was not as healthy and the amniotic fluid which surrounded him in my womb had begun to decrease in volume. For that reason, my obstetric team decided that my baby should be delivered. It was planned that I would receive two doses of steroids in an effort to mature the baby's lungs and delivery was arranged for Friday 15th February, two days time. I was to book into hospital on the morning of February 15 at 8:00am and would be the first patient to be taken to the operating theatre for an elective caesarean section. I opted to have a spinal anaesthetic so I would be awake for the birth.

Stephen and I left for the hospital at 7:30 am. My family were all planning to make their way to the maternity unit for 9:00 am. On the way to the hospital, I rang my mum at home. I kept asking her to promise me that everything was going to be alright, that neither I nor the baby was going to die. She tried to reassure me the best she could. By the time we reached the hospital I had become anxious that the baby was not moving. I lay down on the bed and prodded my stomach. I recall starting to panic, saying to Stephen that the baby had died. Eventually, after what seemed like an eternity but was probably only a few moments, the baby gave an almighty kick. Adrienne arrived at the hospital soon after us and I took the opportunity to hand to her a type written plan, detailing what I wanted to happen to the baby if he was stillborn. I needed to feel in control of the situation, should the worst happen. The plan was an accumulation of all the regrets I had felt when Thomas died, things I wish I had done but was in no fit state to ask for or insist upon. Although I felt quite confident that the baby would be born alive, a part of me could not believe it.

At 09:53 am, baby Joe was born, weighing in at seven pounds two ounces. He was a good weight for thirty-six weeks gestation, but he had not had the opportunity to fatten up in my womb. He was thin, with long stringy arms and legs and a dusting of blonde hair. I can remember the moment of his birth precisely. He was literally lifted out of my womb bawling his head off. To hear our baby cry was such an emotional time for both Stephen and I. I remember saying over and over, "My baby's alive, my baby's alive."

Those words were the complete opposite of what I cried when I first saw Thomas, "My baby's dead."

Twelve members of our friends and family had gathered at the hospital to welcome Joe into the world. It was an intensely emotional time for all. I recall my Nana giving me a huge hug and saying how proud she was of me.

I whispered to her, "Don't forget Thomas will you?"

My worst fear was that with the safe arrival of Joe, everyone would forget that I also had another little boy.

When I was settled on the post-natal ward, I was over-whelmed by the love I felt for Joe. I kept telling everyone he was my angel sent to me from heaven - quite surprising, considering I do not believe in angels or heaven. I had taken a photograph of Thomas into the hospital with me in a little silver frame. My mum placed it on the cabinet next to my bed. I was unable to look at it, I felt so guilty that I was enjoying the presence of Joe. It took nearly two days for me to look at Thomas's picture. When I did, I told him he would always remain my first-born son, I told him how much I loved him and that Joe coming along would not change my feelings for him.

The first evening after a caesarean section, babies are usually taken into the nursery to give their mothers a rest. It is amazing how much a caesarean section can take out of you. Also, you are not mobile as you have a catheter in-situ and are given strong pain relieving medication. When all my family and friends left for the evening, I told the staff I wanted Joe to stay with me throughout the night and no-one dared suggest otherwise. For nearly twelve hours, I held Joe in my arms. I fed him, changed his nappy and hugged him. That night I relished the gift of being able to hold a live and healthy baby, my live and healthy baby. Feeling the warmth radiating from his body and watching the tiny flickers of his facial muscles, filled me with immense relief at what we had accomplished but also immense sadness of what we had lost when Thomas died. It was hard not to compare the two totally different situations, but that evening I could not help but feel on top of the world. Nothing can ever compare to how I felt, holding Joe in my arms. Here I was, holding my live, newborn baby, after nearly two years of unbearable and often soul destroying yearning to care for another baby.

I recovered remarkably well from the caesarean; after all, this was my third. Three days later I was well enough to go home. Apart from a few weepy moments when I was alone in my room, I had not cried during my stay in the hospital. However, when it was time to leave and Joe was settled in his car seat, the one we had planned to take Thomas home in, suddenly from nowhere, tears began to fall. Walking down the corridor accompanied by Stephen, Holly, baby Joe and a midwife, it brought back memories of the last time I had left that very same ward. That time though, I was leaving my baby behind. One of my favourite midwives met me at the doors of the ward. Seeing my distress she put her arms around me and hugged me. She told me that she and the rest of the staff were totally in awe at the way I had coped during my stay. She said they could see how much I adored Joe and how happy he had made me, but they were all wondering when the tears were going to come. The tears they anticipated had definitely arrived; they had taken me by complete surprise. I cried all the way home. I cried for the gift of my two beautiful children, Holly and Joe, but I also cried for myself and my dead baby.

Chapter 15

With Joe around, my life became a hectic time of juggling studying for my degree and being a new mum. At times I was physically exhausted but I felt unable to tell anyone how much I was struggling. How could I complain when I had a live and healthy baby! Initially, I found it impossible to sleep for fear that Joe would be snatched away from me the way Thomas had been. Eventually, we purchased a monitor which sounds an alarm if the baby stops breathing. If I am honest, the first few months of Joe's life were an anxious time for Stephen and I. We were fraught with anguish that he was going to die. Joe became a regular at our GP's surgery and the local Accident and Emergency department and I was forever telephoning NHS Direct. Anything out of the ordinary compelled us to get him checked over. At times I was convinced that they assumed I was a neurotic mother but I did not care. Despite our concerns, Joe thrived and has grown into a beautiful little boy. I am grateful for everyday I share with him and his big sister, Holly. For months I felt a huge amount of guilt that Joe was alive and Thomas wasn't, but over time I have learnt to accept that nothing can ever bring Thomas back. I now believe that Stephen and I deserve to have Joe.

I have since qualified as a teacher. Somehow I believe that if I had not experienced the death of my baby, I would not have got to where I am today. At first, when Thomas died, I almost wished that I had never become pregnant in the first place. If I am truly honest, I even wished that I had miscarried Thomas in the very early weeks. That is not to say that a miscarriage is insignificant, and I would never dismiss the pain and suffering experienced after one but I feel that in the latter months of my pregnancy, I really got to know Thomas, even his personality. I now feel totally different; my outlook on life has changed so much. I would never wish that I did not experience the birth and death of my son. I was totally devastated at first but now I feel he enriched the life of all the people who loved him. All my family and friends have learned to appreciate their own lives much more.

Not only has Thomas had an affect on all the people who love him, but many babies subsequently born at our local maternity unit. I know that changes were made in the maternity unit. Thomas's death and my endless and dignified persistence to find the truth have made the department safeguard against any other deaths. New guidelines were drawn up to inform midwives how to spot potential dangers, particularly dangers involving ante-partum (before birth) bleeding. New procedures were put in place for when midwives needed to report serious incidents. Most importantly, every midwife realised how dangerous it can be to become complacent in their jobs. I will never know if Thomas has directly saved the life of any babies born since he died, but many people have told me he has done and he still will do in the future.

In July, 2002 my mum gave me a bundle of money she had been saving up in secret. It was to buy a bench in front of Thomas's grave. In the crematorium, directly in front of Thomas's rose bush there was a space just big enough to house one bench. All around, other benches are dotted. They are bought by people in memory of their deceased loved ones. These are not your normal garden benches but permanent fixtures in the crematorium gardens; thus, they are very expensive to buy. Unbeknown to me, my mum was really upset whenever she saw me sit on the cold wet grass at Thomas's grave and made it her secret mission to buy a bench for me. It was one of the most fabulous presents I have ever received. I often think of Stephen and I, when we are an old couple, sitting on our bench in front of Thomas's grave.

I have tried to capture my journey from the raw overwhelming pain in the beginning to my acceptance of the death of Thomas in the following poem. I feel it is a stark contrast from the cries for help within the poem I wrote at the beginning of my grieving process.

My memories of you
A tiny life created,
Growing and nurturing within me.
Hopes and dreams for the future,
How beautiful you will be.

My days are now filled with excitement,
Soon my body will set you free.
Free from the warmth of my womb,
Into the love of your family.

When the day of your birth arrives,
Things are not quite what they seem.
Surrounded by the cries of the newborn,
A broken woman lets out a scream.

Although I still cannot believe it,
That heartbroken woman is me.
I cry with a pain in my heart,
I cry for the death of my baby.

My heart fills with despair and pain,
As I cradle my newborn with care.
I feel the warmth leaving his body,
As I put my lips against his soft downy hair.

I whisper, come back to me sweet baby,
Do not leave me now.
I cannot go home without you,
I cannot as I do not know how.

From deep within my soul,
I find the strength to finally say goodbye.
Goodbye to my own baby angel,
Who from conception, was destined to die.

The hardest part of my journey,
Was leaving my baby behind.
With only his bittersweet memory,
Buried within my heart and my mind.

I take each day at a time,
Soon hazy days turn into months and then years.
As I walk the path before me,
With feelings of anger, pain and tears.

I have now found the courage within me,
To help me to finally move on.
I have learned to just live with the memory,
Of my much loved but gone little one.

Chapter 16

As Thomas's sixth birthday passes and this book draws to a close, I feel it is time to explain my reasons for opening my heart and sharing my inner most feelings.

In the immediate months after Thomas died, the loneliness I felt was overwhelming. There are many books written about baby loss and they provide valuable information and support. However, I never came across any that truly captured the journey from the early days, when your sense of loss and grief is at its most intense, to a point where you finally realise that the death of your baby is something which you can learn to live with. I am now at a point in my life where I have learned to live with the pain; it is nowhere near as raw as in the beginning.

When Thomas first died, I felt a physical pain in my heart. I kept telling my family and the medical staff that my heart was hurting and it truly was. That pain is now merely a nagging aching and a yearning to see Thomas just one more time. The phrase 'one more time' has almost become a cliché to me, and I am sure this is the case for many other parents facing this nightmare. I would give anything to see Thomas one more time. I want to hold him and tell him I love him one more time. I want to feel his beautiful soft skin and kiss his chubby lips one more time.

Over the past five years I have watched Sarah's daughter, the baby that was born the day after Thomas, grow into a beautiful little girl. In the beginning everywhere I went I seemed to catch a glimpse of them. Over time I have learned to cope with meeting them. A few years back I saw Sarah, behind her, pedalling furiously on a little tricycle was Megan. I had to stop the car I was driving and watched Megan pedal into the distance. I cried that day because I will never see Thomas ride a bike. Sometimes when I least expect it, I will be overcome by something and the tears will fall.

I have spent many a sleepless night deciding whether to include my experience of being cared for by the midwife who let me down so badly. I eventually decided that my grieving process could not be fully explained without including her actions. I have never set out to take revenge. I feel my story needed to be told. If by opening my heart I manage to help just one mother and father who are struggling to cope with the death of their baby, then my effort has been worthwhile. The midwife still works at the same hospital where Thomas died but she now works in the ante-natal clinic, escorting women in to see their consultant, undertaking urine analysis and other duties performed when women visit their hospital consultant.

Some people say forgiveness is the key to happiness and for that reason; I try so hard not to hate the midwife. I know she never set out to intentionally hurt Thomas. Sometimes I even feel sorry for her because although I have to live the rest of my life without Thomas, I know I did nothing wrong except allow myself to be convinced by someone I trusted that my baby was fine and not in danger. Even though I feel she has not truly paid for her actions, I know she has to live the rest of her life with her conscience and sometimes that can be much harder than any retribution. Below is a letter I wrote to her two years ago, but never felt the courage to send to her. I feel that by sharing the letter, you the reader, can gain an insight into how I feel about the midwife and her actions.

My baby Thomas will be four years old on 18th July. I say 'will be' in the present tense, as he still remains a huge part of our lives and still has a place within our family. Nothing could have prepared me for the huge feeling of overwhelming grief I felt when Thomas died; no-one ever expects to have to arrange the funeral of their child. If I am totally honest, I have been through four years of agonising hell, which I must admit was made immensely worse by the care we received from you. I am not writing this letter just to make accusations and off load any pent up anger; I am merely hoping to finally try to close a huge chapter of my life, in order to move on and look forward to the future.

We both know that our recollections of what occurred on the evening of the 17th July, 2000 differ, and I still stick to what I originally said. I will never accept that your assessment of my situation was correct, and quite rightly, the Trust did identify areas of concern regarding your practice. I have now explored nearly all the options open to me in my quest to secure what I consider to be suitable justice and recognition of the failings in practice which contributed to the death of my baby. The only option left is litigation but that is something I will not pursue. I do not want financial compensation; money has never been our goal. I am now left with the realisation that I will have to live the rest of my life not knowing if a quicker diagnosis and recognition of my condition could have saved Thomas. If you had performed a trace of his heart rate when you said you would, I would have known Thomas was either still alive, with a normal heart rate or maybe he would have been showing signs of distress and an emergency section performed. Either way I do accept that he could have still died, but I would have known that everything which could have been done for him, was.

You never even attempted to visit me soon after Thomas was born, before I told anyone what had happened. I take that to be recognition on your part of possible failings in the care you gave me. You never showed me any compassion over the death of my baby. I know you will never admit that you *did anything wrong, but you never even said sorry to me for the inadequate areas of your care that the Trust identified, or even the fact that I felt there were problems with the way you treated me. You could have written to me, or sent a message to me. I may have ripped up your letter, but you never even tried. You are a mother yourself; can you imagine how it feels to place your own baby into the ground and want to be with him so much that you want to die too?*

I believe that this letter highlights the hurt I felt and still do feel by the way we were treated by the midwife. For a time, I wanted to meet up with her to try to resolve the situation. Only two people know what happened that evening, the midwife and myself. I know I am telling the truth so I wanted the opportunity to hear her version of events for myself. On reflection, I do not feel I would have gained anything from such a meeting. She probably would not have agreed to one anyway.

Chapter 17

I never thought I would ever be able to say this but as I embark on my new teaching career and bask in the love of my husband and two beautiful children, I am happy. In fact I am so happy, that a part of me wonders what is around the corner. What next catastrophe is going to knock me off my feet? I will be forever waiting for it to come but I am sure that if it does, I will cope. Nothing can be worse than walking behind a coffin containing your newborn baby.

Epilogue

Sands reports that seventeen babies are stillborn or die within the first few weeks of life each day in the United Kingdom. Sometimes, as a day draws to a close, I find it difficult to imagine seventeen families are at the start of a devastating grieving process. They are about to embark on a path of unrelenting sadness, guilt, loneliness and pain. In the first few days, it is impossible to imagine the pain will get any easier. You do not even want the pain to ease as it is a link to your baby. I hope you, the reader, can see how I worked through my grief and finally was able to live a normal life once again.

When a family faces the stillbirth of a baby, it is surprising how often people tell you that their mum, friend, or grandma suffered a stillbirth. I am grateful that I was able to spend time with Thomas, to name him, hug and kiss him. Even as late as the 1970s, stillbirth was a taboo subject. Mothers of such babies were not encouraged to hold their dead babies, give them a name or even know the sex. Many such mothers go through life with a short memory of the unusual silence after they delivered their babies and the swift actions of a midwife as she removed the baby, without the mother ever seeing them. It was not done callously; rather it was thought the best for the mother.

Today things have changed. Ultrasound scanning and other advances in medical technology have helped society to see an unborn baby as a human being and an individual in its own right from as early as eight weeks' gestation. Families are now encouraged to spend time with their dead babies. They are encouraged to make memories that will stay with them for a lifetime.

I think I am one of the lucky ones. When I entered the exclusive club, the one you can only become member of when you have lost a child, I took with me a head full of memories, a heart full of acknowledged love and a box of memories containing photographs, hand and footprints and even a lock of hair. I have never had to deny the presence of Thomas.

In February I will be with my best friend, Ragen, when she delivers her second baby. I am honoured to be with her at such an intimate time and aim to be the best birth partner ever. Ragen does not know this, but I am anxious and nervous. When she has delivered a live, healthy baby, I will be so relieved. Despite the fact that seventeen babies a day die, the chances of something going wrong during pregnancy and delivery are very low. However, I now do not take the birth of a live and healthy baby for granted. Each and every one is a miracle.

19th February 2005: Yesterday Ragen gave birth to a healthy and very beautiful baby boy. I was the first human being, other than the obstetrician and the midwife, to hold baby Dylan and will be forever grateful to Ragen and her husband Craig for allowing me to share something special with them.

Finally, to all the families going through this nightmare, take strength from my story, take each day at a time and you will learn to live without your little baby. Over time, the good days will outnumber the bad.

Love Shelley

Sands
Stillbirth & neonatal death charity

In the UK, 17 babies a day are stillborn or die within the first twenty eight days of life; a devastating bereavement for the parents and for their families and friends.

What we do

Sands is a national charity, established by bereaved parents in 1981.

Sands core aims are to:

- Support anyone affected by the death of a baby.

- Improve the quality of care and services bereaved families receive from health professionals following the death of their baby.

- Promote research and changes in practice that could help to reduce the loss of babies' lives.

Sands head office:
Open: 10am-5pm,
Monday to Friday
28 Portland Place
London
W1B 1LY

Helpline: 020 7436 5881
Office: 020 7436 7940
Fax: 020 7436 3715
E mail:
support@uk-sands.org
Website: www.uk-sands.org